Maison fondée en 1862

LADURÉE

Fabricant de douceurs

Paris

Sucré

THE RECIPES

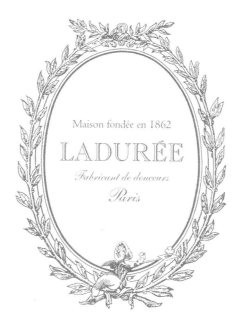

Maison fondée en 1862

LADURÉE

Fabricant de douceurs

Paris

Sucré

THE RECIPES

PASTRY CHEF: PHILIPPE ANDRIEU

PHOTOGRAPHY: SOPHIE TRAMIER

FOOD STYLING: CHRISTÈLE AGEORGES

TRANSLATION: KERRIN ROUSSET

CHÊNE

LADURÉE
Paris

The Story of Ladurée

The wonderful story of Ladurée began in 1862, when Louis Ernest Ladurée first opened a bakery in the very heart of Paris at 16, rue Royale. During this era, the neighbourhood surrounding the Madeleine was rapidly developing into one of the capital's most important and elegant business districts, where the most prestigious artisans in French luxury goods had already begun to take up residence.

Following a fire in 1872, the bakery reopened as a pastry shop, and Jules Cheret, a famous painter and poster designer of that period, was given the responsibility of creating the new décor. At the beginning of the twentieth century, Jeanne Souchard, Ernest Ladurée's wife, came up with the idea of combining two distinct styles: that of the Parisian *café* and the *pâtisserie.* With this, one of the very first Parisian tea salons was born.

In 1993 the potential of this "sleeping beauty" was recognized by David Holder and his father Francis Holder, founder of the Holder Group. With the opening of the Ladurée restaurant and tea salon on the Champs Élysées in 1997, decorated by Jacques Garcia, this Parisian institution became one of the top destinations for local *gourmandises.*

Over a period of fifteen years, David Holder returned Ladurée to a position of grandeur, opening new boutiques in *Printemps,* the famous department store and on Paris's left bank, followed by openings in London, Geneva and Tokyo – always with its famous macaron as its emblem, bringing with it international renown.

Following the rhythm of the seasons, and like the launch of new fashion collections, Pastry Chef Philippe Andrieu creates new flavours twice a year for many of his creations: *les religieuses, les Saint Honoré, les macarons...*

Ladurée is a celebration of all things sweet and feminine: for as many flavours as there are in Philippe's pastries, there is as broad a palette of colours. Delicate pink, vibrant purple and Ladurée's iconic pastel green all contribute to the essence of what is Ladurée, and are a colourful signature of its creations.

As Ladurée states, its ultimate objective is to create *belles choses*, or beautiful things, by giving its many boutiques and creations a strong personality, the stamp of the French lifestyle. Far from culinary trends and designs of the moment, Ladurée is where quality and beauty have always gone hand in hand.

LADURÉE
LADURÉE

Contents

Les Macarons

Macarons

Makes approximately 50 macarons
Preparation: 2 hours *Cooking time: 12 to 15 minutes* *Resting time: minimum of 12 hours*

Macarons Amande

Almond Macarons

Macaron shells
2 ¾ cups + 1 tbsp | 275 g ground almonds (almond flour)
2 cups + 1 tbsp | 250 g confectioners' (icing) sugar
6 egg whites + ½ egg white
1 cup + 1 tbsp | 210 g granulated sugar
1 cup | 100 g chopped almonds

Almond filling
10 ½ tbsp | 150 g butter
1 ½ cups | 320 g almond paste (65% almonds)
4 oz | 120 g unsweetened almond pulp (you can replace with heavy (double) cream)
⅓ cup | 80 ml whipping cream, cold

EQUIPMENT
Piping bag fitted with a ½-inch | 10-mm plain tip

MACARON SHELLS

1 ••• Combine the ground almonds and confectioners' sugar in a food processor and pulse to obtain a fine powder. Sift or strain through a sieve to remove any lumps.

2 ••• In a clean, dry bowl, whisk the 6 egg whites to a foam. Once they are frothy, add a third of the granulated sugar and whip until sugar is dissolved; add another third of the granulated sugar, whip for another minute; finally add the remaining granulated sugar and whip for 1 more minute. Using a rubber spatula, delicately fold the sifted mixture of ground almonds and confectioners' sugar into the whipped egg whites. In a separate small bowl, beat the remaining ½ egg white until just frothy. Then add to the final mixture, folding gently to slightly loosen the batter.

•••

3 ••· Transfer mixture to the piping bag fitted with a plain tip. On a baking sheet lined with parchment paper, pipe small macaron rounds 1 ¼-1 ½ inches | 3-4 cm in diameter. Lightly tap the sheet so the macarons spread fully. Sprinkle chopped almonds on top.
Preheat the oven to 300°F | 150°C | gas mark 2.
Allow the macarons to sit uncovered for 10 minutes and then place in the oven. Bake for approximately 15 minutes until they form a slight crust.

4 ••· Remove baking sheet from the oven, and with a small glass, carefully pour a tiny amount of water in between the sheet and the parchment paper (lift the paper ever so slightly corner by corner). The moisture and steam that result from the water on the hot baking sheet will allow the macarons to peel off more easily once they are cool. Do not pour too much water as this could cause the macarons to become soggy. Allow to cool completely.
Remove half of the macaron shells and place them upside down on a plate.

Almond filling

5 ••· Cut the butter into small pieces. Put in a heatproof bowl set over a pan of gently simmering water or in the microwave oven, and soften until creamy, without allowing it to melt.
In a large bowl, thin the almond paste by mixing it with the almond pulp. Add the chilled cream and the softened butter. Beat on high speed using an electric mixer fitted with the paddle attachment until the mixture is homogenous.

6 ••• Spoon the almond cream into a clean piping bag fitted with a plain tip. Pipe a coin of almond cream onto the macaron shells resting upside down. Top each one with the remaining macaron shells.
Keep macarons in an airtight container in the refrigerator for 12 hours before tasting.

Chef's tips

It is possible that your macaron shells will slightly crack on top for many different reasons. This could be the result of the ingredients, the oven or how the preparation was mixed. Whatever the reason, do not be discouraged! Rest assured: cracked or not, your macarons will be just as delicious. With experience, you will succeed and have beautiful, smooth macarons.

It is strongly recommended that you allow the finished macarons to rest one night in the refrigerator. During this time, a reaction takes place among the ingredients, further enhancing and refining the flavour and texture.

Makes approximately 50 macarons
Preparation: 2 hours *Cooking time: 12 to 15 minutes* *Resting time: minimum of 14 hours*

Macarons Chocolat

Chocolate Macarons

Chocolate ganache
10 oz | 290 g chocolate (minimum 70% cacao solids)
1 cup + 2 tbsp | 270 ml heavy (double) cream
4 tbsp | 60 g butter

Macaron shells
2 ¾ cups | 260 g ground almonds (almond flour)
2 cups + 1 tbsp | 250 g confectioners' (icing) sugar
2 ¾ tbsp (15 g) unsweetened cocoa powder
2 oz | 65 g chocolate (minimum 70% cacao solids)
6 egg whites + ½ egg white
1 cup + 1 tbsp | 210 g granulated sugar

EQUIPMENT
Piping bag fitted with a ½-inch | 10-mm plain tip

CHOCOLATE GANACHE

1 ••• Prepare the ganache. Using a knife, finely chop the chocolate on a cutting board and place in a large bowl. In a saucepan, bring the cream to a boil. Pour the hot cream in 3 parts over the chopped chocolate, mixing with a wooden spatula between each addition to homogenize the preparation.

Cut the butter into small pieces and stir into the ganache until very smooth. Transfer to a baking dish and cover with plastic wrap, so that the plastic is in contact with the ganache. Allow the ganache to cool at room temperature and then refrigerate for 1 hour until it has a thick, creamy consistency.

•••

Macaron shells

2 ••• Combine the ground almonds, confectioners' sugar and cocoa powder in a food processor and pulse to obtain a fine powder. Sift or strain through a sieve to remove any lumps.
Melt the chocolate in a heatproof bowl set over a pan of gently simmering water or in the microwave oven until it is lukewarm (approx. 95°F | 35°C).

3 ••• In a clean, dry bowl, whisk the 6 egg whites to a foam. Once they are frothy, add a third of the granulated sugar and whip until sugar is dissolved; add another third of the granulated sugar, whip for another minute; finally add the remaining granulated sugar and whip for 1 more minute. Pour the melted chocolate over the whipped egg whites. Using a rubber spatula, roughly incorporate the chocolate, and then immediately and delicately fold the sifted mixture of ground almonds, confectioners' sugar and cocoa powder into the chocolate and egg white mixture. In a separate small bowl, beat the remaining ½ egg white until just frothy. Then add to the final mixture, folding gently to slightly loosen the batter.

4 ••• Transfer mixture to the piping bag fitted with a plain tip. On a baking sheet lined with parchment paper, pipe small macaron rounds 1 ¼-1 ½ inches | 3-4 cm in diameter. Lightly tap the sheet so the macarons spread fully.
Preheat the oven to 300°F | 150°C | gas mark 2.
Allow the macarons to sit uncovered for 10 minutes and then place in the oven. Bake for approximately 15 minutes until they form a slight crust.

5 ••• Remove baking sheet from the oven, and with a small glass, carefully pour a tiny amount of water in between the sheet and the parchment paper (lift the paper ever so slightly corner by corner). The moisture and steam that result from the water on the hot baking sheet will allow the macarons to peel off more easily once they are cool. Do not pour too much water as this could cause the macarons to become soggy. Allow to cool completely. Remove half of the macaron shells and place them upside down on a plate.

6 ••• When the ganache has a creamy consistency, pour into a clean piping bag fitted with a plain tip. Pipe a coin of ganache onto the macaron shells resting upside down. Top each with the remaining macaron shells. Keep macarons in an airtight container in the refrigerator for 12 hours before tasting.

Chef's tips

It is possible that your macaron shells will slightly crack on top for many different reasons. This could be the result of the ingredients, the oven or how the preparation was mixed. Whatever the reason, do not be discouraged! Rest assured: cracked or not, your macarons will be just as delicious. With experience, you will succeed and have beautiful, smooth macarons.

It is strongly recommended that you allow the finished macarons to rest one night in the refrigerator. During this time, a reaction takes place among the ingredients, further enhancing and refining the flavour and texture.

Makes approximately 50 macarons
Preparation: 2 ½ hours *Cooking time: 12 to 15 minutes* *Resting time: 24 hours*

Macarons Citron

Lemon Macarons

Lemon cream

¾ cup + 1 tbsp | 160 g granulated sugar
zest of 1 lemon, grated (2 tsp | 5 g)
2 tsp (5 g) cornstarch (cornflour)
3 eggs
½ cup | 110 ml lemon juice
1 cup | 235 g butter, softened

Macaron shells

2 ¾ cups + 1 tbsp | 275 g ground almonds (almond flour)
2 cups + 1 tbsp | 250 g confectioners' (icing) sugar
6 egg whites + ½ egg white
1 cup + 1 tbsp | 210 g granulated sugar
a few drops of yellow food colouring

EQUIPMENT

Piping bag fitted with a ½-inch | 10-mm plain tip

LEMON CREAM

1 ••• Prepare the lemon cream one day ahead.
In a bowl, mix together the sugar and lemon zest. Add the cornstarch, the eggs one at a time and the lemon juice.
Pour this mixture into a saucepan and cook over low heat, stirring with a spatula until it simmers, allowing the cream to thicken.

2 ••• Remove from heat. Allow the cream to cool slightly for approximately 10 minutes, so that it stays hot but not scalding (140°F | 60°C). Add the softened butter. In a blender or food processor, blend the butter and cream together to obtain a homogenous mixture.
Keep in an airtight container in the refrigerator for a minimum of 12 hours to allow the cream to become firm.

•••

Macaron shells

3 ••• Combine the ground almonds and confectioners' sugar in a food processor and pulse to obtain a fine powder. Sift or strain through a sieve to remove any lumps.

4 ••• In a clean, dry bowl, whisk the 6 egg whites to a foam. Once they are frothy, add a third of the granulated sugar and whip until sugar is dissolved; add another third of the granulated sugar, whip for another minute; finally add the remaining granulated sugar and whip for 1 more minute. Using a clean rubber spatula, delicately fold the sifted mixture of ground almonds and confectioners' sugar into the whipped egg whites. Add a few drops of food colouring to obtain the desired colour. In a separate small bowl, beat the remaining ½ egg white until just frothy. Then add to the final mixture, folding gently to slightly loosen the batter.

5 ••• Transfer the mixture to the piping bag fitted with a plain tip. On a baking sheet lined with parchment paper, pipe small macaron rounds 1 ¼-1 ½ inches | 3-4 cm in diameter. Lightly tap the sheet so the macarons spread fully.
Preheat the oven to 300°F | 150°C | gas mark 2.
Allow the macarons to sit uncovered for 10 minutes and then place in the oven. Bake for approximately 15 minutes until they form a slight crust.

6 ••• Remove baking sheet from the oven, and with a small glass, carefully pour a tiny amount of water in between the sheet and the parchment paper (lift the paper ever so slightly corner by corner). The moisture and steam that result from the water on the hot baking sheet will allow the macarons to peel off more easily once they are cool. Do not pour too much water as this could cause the macarons to become soggy. Allow to cool completely.
Remove half of the macaron shells and place them upside down on a plate.

7 ••• Spoon the lemon cream into a clean piping bag fitted with a plain tip. Pipe a coin of lemon cream onto the macaron shells resting upside down. Top each with the remaining macaron shells.
Keep macarons in an airtight container in the refrigerator for 12 hours before tasting.

Chef's tips

It is possible that your macaron shells will slightly crack on top for many different reasons. This could be the result of the ingredients, the oven or how the preparation was mixed. Whatever the reason, do not be discouraged! Rest assured: cracked or not, your macarons will be just as delicious. With experience, you will succeed and have beautiful, smooth macarons.

It is strongly recommended that you allow the finished macarons to rest one night in the refrigerator. During this time, a reaction takes place among the ingredients, further enhancing and refining the flavour and texture.

Makes approximately 50 macarons
Preparation: 2 hours *Cooking time: 12 to 15 minutes* *Resting time: minimum of 12 hours*

Macarons Framboise

Raspberry Macarons

Raspberry jam
1 cup + 2 tbsp | 225 g granulated sugar
2 tsp pectin (powder)
3 cups | 375 g fresh raspberries
½ lemon

Macaron shells
2 ¾ cups + 1 tbsp | 275 g ground almonds (almond flour)
2 cups + 1 tbsp | 250 g confectioners' (icing) sugar
6 egg whites + ½ egg white
1 cup + 1 tbsp | 210 g granulated sugar
a few drops of red food colouring

Equipment
Piping bag fitted with a ½-inch | 10-mm plain tip

Raspberry jam

1 ••• In a large bowl, mix together the sugar and pectin.
Place the raspberries in a saucepan and puree them using an immersion hand blender. Turn heat to low and bring the puree to lukewarm. Add the sugar and pectin mixture, as well as the juice from the lemon half. Over medium heat, bring to a boil and cook for 2 minutes.

2 ••• Pour the jam into a large bowl and cover with plastic wrap. Allow to cool completely and then place in the refrigerator.

Macaron shells

3 ••• Combine the ground almonds and confectioners' sugar in a food processor and pulse to obtain a fine powder. Sift or strain through a sieve to remove any lumps.

•••

4 ••• In a clean, dry bowl, whisk the 6 egg whites to a foam. Once they are frothy, add a third of the granulated sugar and whip until sugar is dissolved; add another third of the granulated sugar, whip for another minute; finally add the remaining granulated sugar and whip for 1 more minute. Using a rubber spatula, delicately fold the sifted mixture of ground almonds and confectioners' sugar into the whipped egg whites. Add a few drops of food colouring to obtain the desired colour. In a separate small bowl, beat the remaining ½ egg white until just frothy. Then add to the final mixture, folding gently to slightly loosen the batter.

5 ••• Transfer the mixture to the piping bag fitted with a plain tip. On a baking sheet lined with parchment paper, pipe small macaron rounds 1 ¼-1 ½ inches | 3-4 cm in diameter. Lightly tap the sheet so the macarons spread fully.

Preheat the oven to 300°F | 150°C | gas mark 2.

Allow the macarons to sit uncovered for 10 minutes and then place in the oven. Bake for approximately 15 minutes until they form a slight crust.

6 ••• Remove baking sheet from the oven, and with a small glass, carefully pour a tiny amount of water in between the sheet and the parchment paper (lift the paper ever so slightly corner by corner). The moisture and steam that result from the water on the hot baking sheet will allow the macarons to peel off more easily once they are cool. Do not pour too much water as this could cause the macarons to become soggy. Allow to cool completely.

Remove half of the macaron shells and place them upside down on a plate.

7 ••• Spoon the raspberry jam into a clean piping bag fitted with a plain tip. Pipe a coin of raspberry jam onto the macaron shells resting upside down. Top each with the remaining macaron shells.
Keep macarons in an airtight container in the refrigerator for 12 hours before tasting.

Chef's tips

It is possible that your macaron shells will slightly crack on top for many different reasons. This could be the result of the ingredients, the oven or how the preparation was mixed. Whatever the reason, do not be discouraged! Rest assured: cracked or not, your macarons will be just as delicious. With experience, you will succeed and have beautiful, smooth macarons.

It is strongly recommended that you allow the finished macarons to rest one night in the refrigerator. During this time, a reaction takes place among the ingredients, further enhancing and refining the flavour and texture.

Les Petits Gâteaux

Little Cakes

Makes 8 savarins
Preparation: 2 ½ hours + basic recipe *Cooking time: 25 minutes* *Resting time: 1 hour*

Savarins

Savarins

Baba dough
½ oz | 12 g fresh yeast
2 tbsp (20 g) water
2 cups | 250 g cake flour
1 pinch of fleur de sel (or other coarse sea salt)
1 ¼ tbsp (15 g) granulated sugar
4 eggs
5 tbsp | 75 g butter
+ 1 ½ tbsp butter for moulds

Rum syrup
4 ¼ cups | 1 litre water
1 ¼ cups | 250 g granulated sugar
1 lemon, unwaxed
1 orange, unwaxed
1 vanilla bean
½ cup | 120 ml aged rum (rhum agricole if possible)
+ ½ cup | 125 ml aged rum for finish

Sweetened whipped cream
2 ¾ cups | 325 g sweetened whipped cream: see basic recipe

Seasonal fruits for decoration

EQUIPMENT
8 savarin moulds, 2 ¾-inch | 7-cm diameter rings
Piping bag without tip
Piping bag fitted with a ½-inch | 10-mm star tip

BABA DOUGH

1 ••• Cut the butter into small pieces and allow to soften at room temperature. Break the yeast into small pieces with your fingers and dilute in the water at room temperature. In a large bowl, place the flour, salt and sugar. Add the diluted yeast and 2 eggs, and start to mix with a wooden spatula until the dough pulls away from the sides of the bowl. Add 1 egg, knead until it pulls away from the sides of the bowl again, and repeat this process with the last egg. Incorporate the softened butter and continue to work in to the dough until it once again pulls away from the sides of the bowl.

•••

2 ••· Cover the dough with a damp dish towel or plastic wrap. Allow the dough to double in volume at room temperature (approximately 1 hour).

3 ••· Preheat the oven to 340°F | 170°C | gas mark 3.
Butter the moulds. Transfer dough to the piping bag without tip and fill moulds. Allow the dough to double in volume and rise up to the edges of the moulds. Place in oven and bake for 20 minutes.

Rum syrup

4 ••· Pour the water and sugar into a saucepan. Using a vegetable peeler, remove the zest of the lemon and orange (avoiding the bitter white pith). Juice both citrus fruits. With a sharp knife, slice the vanilla bean in half lengthwise. Using the tip, scrape the interior to remove the seeds.
Add the vanilla pod, vanilla seeds, pressed citrus juice and zest to the saucepan with the water and sugar. Bring to a boil. Remove from heat, strain through a fine mesh sieve to discard all solids, and add the rum.

5 ••· Transfer the syrup to a baking dish that is large enough to hold the baked savarins. Turn pastries around in the syrup, dipping the tops and bottoms, until well soaked. Place a wire rack on a large dish or rimmed baking sheet, and place savarins on the rack. Reheat the remaining syrup and when hot, drizzle over the cakes several times. Allow to cool.

Chef's tip
If you have a stand mixer, prepare the dough in the bowl of the mixer fitted with the dough hook attachment. You can also mix the ingredients in a food processor.

Assembly

6 ••· Place savarins on a serving platter and drizzle generously with rum. Using the piping bag fitted with a star tip, top each cake with sweetened whipped cream. Decorate with seasonal fruits.

Makes 8 barquettes
Preparation: 2 hours + basic recipes *Cooking time: 30 minutes* *Resting time: 1 ½ hours*

Barquettes aux Marrons

Chestnut Barquettes

Sweet almond pastry for barquette shells
7 oz | 200 g dough: see basic recipe
2 tbsp butter for moulds
2 ½ tbsp all-purpose flour for work surface

Almond cream
5 oz | 150 g almond cream: see basic recipe

Chestnut cream
7 tbsp | 100 g butter
7 oz | 200 g chestnut paste
1 tbsp dark rum
2 ½ tbsp (40 ml) heavy (double) cream

Assembly
2 tbsp dark rum
3 oz | 80 g chestnut pieces

Milk chocolate glaze
4 ½ oz | 125 g milk chocolate
⅓ cup | 75 ml heavy (double) cream

EQUIPMENT
Barquette moulds, 3 ½ x 1 ½-inch | 9 x 4-cm
Piping bag fitted with a ½-inch | 10-mm plain tip
Piping bag fitted with a ⅛-inch | 3-mm star tip
Rolling pin
Pastry brush

SWEET ALMOND PASTRY FOR BARQUETTE SHELLS

1 ••• Prepare the dough one day ahead (see basic recipe).
The following day, melt the butter in a small saucepan over low heat, and butter the moulds with a pastry brush. Keep in the refrigerator.

•••

2 ••· Meanwhile, roll out the dough to 1⁄10 inch | 2 mm thick on a floured work surface, and fit into moulds. Use a small piece of dough dredged in flour to push the rolled dough against the sides. Using a rolling pin, roll over the edges to remove any overhang. Allow the dough to rest for 1 hour in the refrigerator.

Almond cream

3 ••· Preheat the oven to 340°F | 170°C | gas mark 3.
Prepare the almond cream (see basic recipe).
Transfer almond cream to the piping bag fitted with a plain tip. Fill the barquettes to 1⁄10 inch | 2 mm below the edge of the pastry shell.
Place in oven and bake for approximately 30 minutes until golden.
Remove from oven, allow to cool completely and remove from the moulds.

Chestnut cream

4 ••· Cut the butter into small pieces. Put in a heatproof bowl set over a pan of gently simmering water or in the microwave to soften until creamy, without allowing it to melt.
In a large bowl, mix the chestnut paste until homogenous. Add the rum and softened butter. Beat on high speed with an electric mixer fitted with the paddle attachment to emulsify the mixture. Pour in the heavy cream and continue to mix. Assemble barquettes immediately.

Assembly

5 ••· Using a pastry brush, lightly soak the surface of the baked almond cream with rum. Using a palette knife (or offset spatula), place a small amount of chestnut cream on the almond cream. Arrange 3 or 4 crumbled chestnut pieces on top of each pastry. Using the palette knife, cover with chestnut cream, giving it the same shape as the base, and create a well-pronounced ridge lengthwise across the top. Freeze for 30 minutes.

Milk chocolate glaze

6 ••· Using a knife, chop the milk chocolate on a cutting board.
In a saucepan, bring the heavy cream to a boil and pour over the chopped chocolate. Carefully stir together. Allow to cool to lukewarm and then using the palette knife, coat the tops of the barquettes.
Spoon the remaining chestnut cream into the piping bag fitted with a star tip, and decorate the ridges with a thin line of cream.

Makes 10 éclairs

Preparation: 1 hour and 15 minutes + basic recipes *Cooking time: 40 minutes* *Resting time: 2 hours*

Éclairs Vanille

Vanilla Éclairs

Crisp sweet pastry for éclair tops

7 tbsp | 100 g butter, very cold
+ 1 ½ tbsp butter for baking sheet
1 cup | 125 g cake flour
½ cup + 2 tbsp | 125 g granulated sugar
1 pinch of vanilla powder (or a few drops of vanilla extract)

Lightened pastry cream

5 cups | 600 g pastry cream: see basic recipe
½ cup | 125 ml heavy (double) cream

Éclairs

Choux pastry: see basic recipe
1 ½ tbsp butter for baking sheet

Confectioners' (icing) sugar for dusting

Equipment

Rolling pin
Piping bag fitted with a ½-inch | 10-mm plain tip
Piping bag fitted with a ⅓-inch | 8-mm plain tip

Crisp sweet pastry for éclair tops

1 ••• Cut the chilled butter into small pieces. In a large bowl, mix the flour, sugar, vanilla and butter until homogenous. If you have a stand mixer, you can prepare the dough in the bowl of the mixer fitted with the paddle attachment. Refrigerate for 1 hour.

2 ••• Roll out the dough between two sheets of parchment paper, as thin as possible (1 mm).
Transfer the rolled dough to a tray and refrigerate for 1 hour or freeze until firm. Remove the top sheet of parchment paper and slice rectangular strips of pastry 5 x ¾-inch | 12 x 2-cm.
Keep pastry in the refrigerator on the parchment paper-lined tray. It will be easier to remove the strips and place on top of the éclairs.

•••

Pastry cream

3 ••• Prepare the pastry cream (see basic recipe) and keep in the refrigerator.

Éclairs

4 ••• Prepare the choux pastry (see basic recipe).
Preheat the oven to 350°F | 180°C | gas mark 4.
Transfer the dough to the piping bag fitted with the ½-inch | 10-mm plain tip. Pipe 5-inch | 12-cm long strips onto a buttered baking sheet. Place a chilled strip of crisp sweet pastry on top of each piped éclair.

5 ••• Place in oven and bake. After 8 to 10 minutes, when they will have started to puff up, open the oven door very slightly, about ⅛ inch | 2-3 mm, to allow steam to escape. Bake the éclairs for approximately 30 minutes with the oven door slightly ajar, until golden. (You can slip the handle of a wooden spoon into the oven to keep ajar.)
Remove éclairs from oven and allow to cool on a wire rack.

Lightened pastry cream

6 ••• Keep the heavy cream in the refrigerator until ready to use. Place a large mixing bowl in the freezer to chill. Pour the heavy cream into the chilled bowl and whisk energetically until it thickens and becomes firm. Whisk the chilled pastry cream in another bowl until smooth, eliminating any lumps. Using a rubber spatula, gently fold the whipped cream into the pastry cream.

Filling

7 ••• Using the ⅓-inch | 8-mm plain tip without the piping bag, poke 3 holes in the base of each éclair, one in the center and the others ¾ inch | 2 cm from each end. The strips of crisp sweet pastry should be on the other side (top). Transfer the lightened pastry cream to the piping bag fitted with the ⅓-inch | 8-mm plain tip. Fill the cooled éclairs by piping cream into the holes. Dust the tops with confectioners' sugar.

Makes 10 éclairs
Preparation: 1 hour and 15 minutes + basic recipes   *Cooking time: 40 minutes*

Éclairs Chocolat

Chocolate Éclairs

Éclairs
Choux pastry: see basic recipe
1 ½ tbsp butter for baking sheet

Chocolate pastry cream
3 ¾ cups | 450 g pastry cream: see basic recipe
4 oz | 120 g chocolate (70% cacao solids)
¾ cup + 1 ½ tbsp | 200 ml whole milk

Chocolate fondant
7 oz | 200 g white pouring fondant
2 ½ oz | 70 g chocolate (80% cacao solids)
1 tbsp water
⅓ cup | 60 g granulated sugar

Equipment
Piping bag fitted with a ½-inch | 10-mm plain tip
Piping bag fitted with a ⅓-inch | 8-mm plain tip

Pastry cream

1 ••• Prepare the pastry cream (see basic recipe) and keep in the refrigerator.

Éclairs

2 ••• Prepare the choux pastry (see basic recipe).
Preheat the oven to 350°F | 180°C | gas mark 4.
Transfer the dough to the piping bag fitted with the ½-inch | 10-mm plain tip. On a buttered baking sheet, pipe 5-inch | 12-cm long strips.

3 ••• Place in oven and bake. After 8 to 10 minutes, when they will have started to puff up, open the oven door very slightly, about ⅛ inch | 2-3 mm, to allow steam to escape. Bake the éclairs for approximately 30 minutes with the oven door slightly ajar, until golden. (You can slip the handle of a wooden spoon into the oven to keep ajar.)
Remove éclairs from oven and allow to cool on a wire rack. •••

Chocolate pastry cream

4 ••• Remove pastry cream from the refrigerator and pour into a large bowl. Whisk until smooth, eliminating any lumps.

Using a knife, chop the chocolate on a cutting board and place in another large bowl. In a saucepan, bring the milk to a boil and pour over the chopped chocolate. Stir together. Once again, whisk the pastry cream until smooth and incorporate the milk and chocolate mixture (ganache) until homogenous. Refrigerate for 30 minutes until firm.

Filling

5 ••• Using the ⅓-inch | 8-mm plain tip without the piping bag, poke 3 holes in the base of each éclair, one in the center and the others ¾ inch | 2 cm from each end. Transfer the chocolate pastry cream to the piping bag fitted with the ⅓-inch | 8-mm plain tip. Fill the cooled éclairs by piping cream into the holes.

Chocolate fondant

6 ••• Place the pouring fondant in a heatproof bowl set over a pan of gently simmering water, stirring occasionally to soften.

Meanwhile, using a knife, chop the chocolate on a cutting board and place in another heatproof bowl. When the fondant is lukewarm, remove from heat and put the bowl of chocolate over the simmering water in its place to melt.

In a saucepan, bring the water and sugar to a boil to obtain a syrup.

Mix the melted chocolate into the softened fondant.

Add the syrup and stir until smooth.

Dip the tops of the éclairs into this preparation to glaze and allow to cool.

Chef's tip

Prepare your éclairs in advance so that a positive reaction takes place between the pastry shell and the pastry cream.

Makes 25 to 30 cream puffs

Preparation: 1 hour and 15 minutes + basic recipes *Cooking time: 40 minutes*

Choux à la Rose

Rose Cream Puffs

Cream puffs

Choux pastry: see basic recipe

1 ½ tbsp butter for baking sheet

Rose pastry cream

3 ⅓ cups | 400 g pastry cream: see basic recipe

1 tbsp rose water

2 tbsp rose syrup

3 drops natural rose essential oil

Rose fondant

3 oz | 80 g white chocolate

4 oz | 120 g white pouring fondant

5 tbsp rose syrup

4 drops natural rose essential oil

a few drops of red food colouring

25 to 30 raspberries for decoration

EQUIPMENT

Piping bag fitted with a ½-inch | 10-mm plain tip

Piping bag fitted with a ⅓-inch | 8-mm plain tip

PASTRY CREAM

1 ••• Prepare the pastry cream (see basic recipe) and keep in the refrigerator.

CREAM PUFFS

2 ••• Prepare the choux pastry (see basic recipe).
Preheat the oven to 350°F | 180°C | gas mark 4.
Transfer the dough to the piping bag fitted with the ½-inch | 10-mm plain tip. Pipe 1 ½-inch | 4-cm diameter choux onto a buttered baking sheet.

•••

3 ••· Place in oven and bake. After 8 to 10 minutes, when they will have started to puff up, open the oven door very slightly, about ⅛ inch | 2-3 mm, to allow steam to escape. Bake the choux for approximately 30 minutes with the oven door slightly ajar, until golden. (You can slip the handle of a wooden spoon into the oven to keep ajar.)
Remove from the oven and allow to cool on a wire rack.

Rose pastry cream

4 ••· Remove pastry cream from the refrigerator. Whisk until smooth, eliminating any lumps, and add the rose water, syrup and essential oil.

Filling

5 ••· Using the ⅓-inch | 8-mm plain tip without the piping bag, poke a hole in the bottom of each cream puff.
Transfer the rose pastry cream to the piping bag fitted with the ⅓-inch | 8-mm plain tip. Fill the cooled cream puffs by piping cream into the holes.

Rose fondant

6 ••· Melt the white chocolate in a heatproof bowl set over a pan of gently simmering water or in the microwave at medium power. In a saucepan, slightly warm the pouring fondant with the syrup and essential oil, and add the melted white chocolate. Add a few drops of food colouring to obtain the desired colour. Stir until smooth.
Dip the tops of the cream puffs into this preparation to glaze and decorate with a raspberry. Allow to set and keep in the refrigerator.

Makes 25 mini salambos
Preparation: 1 hour and 15 minutes + basic recipes *Cooking time: 40 minutes*

Salambos à la Pistache

Pistachio Salambos

Salambos
Choux pastry: see basic recipe
1 ½ tbsp butter for baking sheet

Pistachio pastry cream
3 ⅓ cups | 400 g pastry cream: see basic recipe
1 ½ tbsp (25 g) pistachio paste

Pistachio fondant
4 ½ oz | 125 g white pouring fondant
1 tbsp water
2 tbsp (30 g) pistachio paste
3 oz | 80 g white chocolate

Pistachios, shelled for decoration

Equipment

Piping bag fitted with a ½-inch | 10-mm plain tip
Piping bag fitted with a ⅓-inch | 8-mm plain tip

Pastry cream

1 ••• Prepare the pastry cream (see basic recipe) and keep in the refrigerator.

Salambos

2 ••• Prepare the choux pastry (see basic recipe).
Preheat the oven to 350°F | 180°C | gas mark 4.
Transfer the dough to the piping bag fitted with the ½-inch | 10-mm plain tip. Pipe small strips 2 ⅓ inches | 6 cm long onto a buttered baking sheet.

•••

3 ••· Place in oven and bake. After 8 to 10 minutes, when they will have started to puff up, open the oven door very slightly, about ⅛ inch | 2-3 mm, to allow steam to escape. Bake for approximately 30 minutes with the oven door slightly ajar, until golden. (You can slip the handle of a wooden spoon into the oven to keep ajar.)

Remove salambos from the oven and allow to cool on a wire rack.

Pistachio pastry cream

4 ••· Remove pastry cream from the refrigerator. Whisk until smooth, eliminating any lumps, and incorporate the pistachio paste.

Filling

5 ••· Using the ⅓-inch | 8-mm plain tip without the piping bag, poke a hole in the bottom of each pastry.

Transfer the pistachio pastry cream to the piping bag fitted with the ⅓-inch | 8-mm plain tip. Fill the cooled salambos by piping cream into the holes.

Chef's tip

If the pistachio paste does not bring enough colour to the fondant, you can add 2 to 3 drops of green food colouring.

Pistachio fondant

6 ••· Melt the white chocolate in a heatproof bowl set over a pan of gently simmering water or in the microwave at medium power. In a saucepan, slightly warm the pouring fondant with the water. Add the pistachio paste and the melted white chocolate. Stir until smooth.

Dip the tops of the salambos into this preparation to glaze and decorate with a pistachio. Allow to set and keep in the refrigerator.

Makes 8 individual millefeuilles *Preparation: 2 hours* *Cooking time: 45 minutes*

Millefeuilles Fraise ou Framboise

Strawberry or Raspberry Millefeuilles (Napoleons)

Caramelized puff pastry

See basic recipe

Vanilla mousseline cream

9 tbsp | 125 g butter

1 vanilla bean

1 cup + 1 tbsp | 250 ml whole milk

2 egg yolks

⅓ cup + 1 tbsp | 75 g granulated sugar

3 tbsp (25 g) cornstarch (cornflour)

18 oz | 500 g strawberries or raspberries

EQUIPMENT

Piping bag fitted with a ½-inch | 10-mm plain tip

CARAMELIZED PUFF PASTRY

1 ••• Prepare the caramelized puff pastry (see basic recipe) to obtain 24 rectangles, 3 ½ x 2-inch | 9 x 5-cm.

VANILLA MOUSSELINE CREAM

2 ••• Remove the butter from the refrigerator to soften.
With a sharp knife, slice the vanilla bean in half lengthwise. Using the tip, scrape the interior to remove the seeds. Pour the milk into a saucepan and add the vanilla pod and seeds. Bring to a simmer. Remove from heat, cover immediately and allow to infuse for 15 minutes.

3 ••• In a large bowl, whisk the egg yolks and sugar until slightly pale. Incorporate the cornstarch. Remove the vanilla pod from the milk and put saucepan back over heat, bringing to a simmer. Pour a third of the hot milk over the mixture of egg yolks, sugar and cornstarch (to temper

•••

the yolks). Whisk together and pour the whole mixture back into the saucepan. Bring to a boil while stirring with a whisk, making sure to scrape down the sides of the pan with a spatula.

4 ••• Remove custard from heat and allow to cool for 10 minutes so that it is hot but not boiling. Incorporate half of the butter. Pour into a baking dish, cover with plastic wrap and allow to cool.

5 ••• Meanwhile, wash the strawberries (or raspberries) and drain on a dish towel. Hull strawberries, slice in half and set aside.

Final steps for vanilla mousseline cream and assembly

6 ••• Cut out 24 rectangles of the caramelized puff pastry, 3 ½ x 2-inch | 9 x 5-cm.
The mousseline cream should be at room temperature. If it is still hot, refrigerate for 10 minutes to cool completely.
In a large bowl using an electric mixer, whip the mousseline cream until smooth. Add the remaining half of the butter and beat until emulsified and smooth.

7 ••• Transfer the mousseline cream to the piping bag fitted with a plain tip. Pipe an even layer of cream onto 8 puff pastry rectangles. Arrange strawberry slices (or raspberries) on top and cover with cream. Top with a second layer of puff pastry rectangles, gently settling the pastry on the filling. Repeat the above steps. Keep millefeuilles in the refrigerator.
Serve millefeuilles with coulis and ice cream or sweetened whipped cream.

Makes 12 gourmet delights
Preparation: 1 hour and 15 minutes + basic recipes *Cooking time: 40 minutes*

Plaisirs Gourmands

Gourmet Delights

Cream puffs
Choux pastry: see basic recipe
1 ½ tbsp butter for baking sheet
1 cup | 100 g chopped almonds

Lightened pastry cream
4 cups | 500 g pastry cream: see basic recipe
½ cup - 1 tbsp | 100 ml heavy (double) cream

Sweetened whipped cream
2 ½ cups | 300 g sweetened whipped cream: see basic recipe

26 ½ oz | 750 g strawberries
(or 17 ½ oz | 500 g raspberries)

Confectioners' (icing) sugar for dusting

EQUIPMENT
Piping bag fitted with a ½-inch | 14-mm plain tip
Piping bag fitted with a ⅓-inch | 8-mm plain tip
Piping bag fitted with a ½-inch | 10-mm star tip

PASTRY CREAM

1 ••• Prepare the pastry cream (see basic recipe) and keep in the refrigerator.

CREAM PUFFS

2 ••• Prepare the choux pastry (see basic recipe).
Preheat the oven to 350°F | 180°C | gas mark 4.
Transfer the dough to the piping bag fitted with the ½-inch | 14-mm plain tip. Pipe large choux, oval-shaped (like boudoir biscuits) 3 inches | 8 cm long onto a buttered baking sheet. Lightly sprinkle over the top with the chopped almonds.

•••

3 ••• Place in oven and bake. After 8 to 10 minutes, when they will have started to puff up, open the oven door very slightly, about ⅛ inch | 2-3 mm, to allow steam to escape. Bake for approximately 30 minutes with the oven door slightly ajar, until golden. (You can slip the handle of a wooden spoon into the oven to keep ajar.)
Remove from the oven and allow to cool on a wire rack.

Lightened pastry cream

4 ••• Keep the heavy cream in the refrigerator until ready to use. Place a large mixing bowl in the freezer to chill. Pour the heavy cream into the chilled bowl and whip energetically until it thickens and becomes firm. Whisk the chilled pastry cream in another bowl until smooth, eliminating any lumps. Using a rubber spatula, gently fold in the whipped cream.

Filling

5 ••• Prepare the sweetened whipped cream (see basic recipe) and keep in the refrigerator.

6 ••• Wash the strawberries and drain on a dish towel. Hull and slice in half lengthwise.

7 ••• Carefully cut off the top third of each pastry, slicing horizontally to obtain a base and top. Transfer the lightened pastry cream to the piping bag fitted with the ⅓-inch | 8-mm plain tip. Pipe cream onto the bases. Cut the strawberry halves in two and arrange on top of the cream.
Spoon the sweetened whipped cream into the piping bag fitted with a star tip. Pipe over the strawberries and cover with cream puff tops. Dust with confectioners' sugar.

Makes 10 to 12 Paris-Brest
Preparation: 1 ½ hours + basic recipes *Cooking time: 30 minutes* *Resting time: 40 minutes*

Paris-Brest Individuels

Individual Paris-Brest

Choux pastry

21 oz | 600 g choux pastry: see basic recipe
¾ cup | 70 g sliced (flaked) almonds

Caramelized almonds and hazelnuts

See recipe for praline millefeuille, page 222

Praline mousseline cream

See basic recipe

Confectioners' (icing) sugar for dusting

EQUIPMENT

Piping bag fitted with a ½-inch | 14-mm star tip

CHOUX PASTRY

1 ••• Line a baking sheet with parchment paper. Draw 12 circles on the paper with a 2 ¾-inch | 7-cm diameter, to serve as guide for piping the pastry.
Prepare the choux pastry (see basic recipe).
Preheat the oven to 350°F | 180°C | gas mark 4.
Transfer the dough to the piping bag fitted with a star tip. Pipe rings of dough following the drawn circles on the parchment paper. Gently press down on the dough to spread and widen each base. Sprinkle with sliced almonds.

2 ••• Place sheet in oven and bake. After 8 to 10 minutes, when they will have started to puff up, open the oven door very slightly, about ⅛ inch | 2-3 mm, to allow steam to escape. Bake for approximately 30 minutes with the oven door slightly ajar, until golden. (You can slip the handle of a wooden spoon into the oven to keep ajar.)
Remove Paris-Brest from oven and allow to cool on a wire rack.

•••

Caramelized almonds and hazelnuts

3 ••• Prepare the almonds and hazelnuts (see recipe for praline millefeuille, page 222).

Praline mousseline cream

4 ••• Prepare the mousseline cream (see basic recipe).

Assembly

5 ••• Carefully slice the cooled pastry rings horizontally to obtain a base and top.

Transfer mousseline cream to the piping bag fitted with a star tip, and pipe a thin layer of cream onto the pastry bases. Sprinkle the crushed caramelized almonds and hazelnuts over the cream. Pipe 2 circles of cream over the nuts, lightly pressing down and spreading out the cream.

Cover the Paris-Brest with their pastry tops.

Dust with confectioners' sugar and keep in the refrigerator.

Les Desserts Glacés et Fruités

Frozen & Fruit Desserts

Makes 1 ½ pints | ¾ litre of ice cream *Preparation: 1 ½ hours* *Resting time: 3 hours*

Crème Glacée à la Verveine

Verbena Ice Cream

1 oz | 30 g fresh verbena leaves
1 ⅔ cups | 400 ml whole milk
1 cup + 1 tbsp | 250 ml heavy (double) cream
6 egg yolks
¾ cup | 150 g granulated sugar

Equipment
Ice cream maker

1 ••• Rinse and drain the fresh verbena leaves, discarding any stems. Roughly chop the leaves in thirds.
In a saucepan, bring the milk and about ½ cup | 125 ml of heavy cream to a boil. Remove from heat. Add the verbena leaves, cover and steep for 20 minutes.

2 ••• In a large bowl, whisk the egg yolks and sugar until slightly pale. Strain the milk and cream mixture into a bowl to remove the verbena leaves. Return the liquid to the saucepan and reheat. Pour a third of this hot liquid over the egg yolks and sugar (to temper the yolks). Stir together with a whisk and pour the whole mixture back into the saucepan.

3 ••• Cook over low heat, stirring constantly with a wooden spoon until the custard thickens. It should coat the spoon when ready; if you run your finger down the back of the spoon, the custard should not run back into the line. Important: the custard should never come to a boil. (It should cook at a maximum of 185°F | 85°C.)

•••

4 ••• As soon as the custard has this consistency, remove from heat and add the remaining ½ cup | 125 ml of heavy cream to stop the cooking. Pour into a bowl and continue to stir for 5 minutes so that the custard stays smooth. Refrigerate until chilled.

5 ••• Pour the preparation into the bowl of an ice cream maker and freeze according to the manufacturer's instructions.
When the ice cream is ready, transfer to an airtight container and store in the freezer.

Chef's tips

Churn the ice cream 3 hours before serving for the texture to be at its best. It will keep well for several days in the freezer; simply remove 10 minutes before serving to soften.

As in the preparation of pouring custard (crème anglaise): in the 3rd step above, if you let the custard cook a little too long, lumps will appear. This is due to the egg yolks that are beginning to curdle. To save it, pour into a blender or food processor and briefly blend just to homogenize. Do not blend too long or the custard will liquefy.

Makes 1 quart | 1 litre of ice cream *Preparation: 1 ½ hours* *Resting time: 3 hours*

Glace Pétales de Roses

Rose Petal Ice Cream

2 cups + 2 tbsp | 500 ml whole milk
½ cup | 120 ml heavy (double) cream
3 ½ tbsp (70 ml) rose syrup
3 ⅓ tbsp (50 ml) rose water
8 egg yolks
⅔ cup | 135 g granulated sugar
6 drops natural rose essential oil

Equipment
Ice cream maker

1 ••• In a saucepan, bring the milk and cream to a boil. Remove from heat and add the rose syrup and rose water.

2 ••• In a large bowl, whisk the egg yolks and sugar until slightly pale. Pour a third of the milk and cream mixture over the egg yolks and sugar (to temper the yolks). Stir together with a whisk and pour the whole mixture back into the saucepan.

3 ••• Cook over low heat, stirring constantly with a wooden spoon until the custard thickens. It should coat the spoon when ready; if you run your finger down the back of the spoon, the custard should not run back into the line. Important: the custard should never come to a boil. (It should cook at a maximum of 185°F | 85°C.)

•••

4 ••• As soon as the custard has this consistency, remove from heat and pour into a bowl to stop the cooking. Continue to stir for 5 minutes so that the custard stays smooth.
Incorporate the rose essential oil. Refrigerate until chilled.
Pour the preparation into the bowl of an ice cream maker and freeze according to the manufacturer's instructions.
When the ice cream is ready, transfer to an airtight container and store in the freezer.

Chef's tips

Churn the ice cream 3 hours before serving for the texture to be at its best. It will keep well for several days in the freezer; simply remove 10 minutes before serving to soften.

As in the preparation of pouring custard (crème anglaise): in the 3rd step above, if you let the custard cook a little too long, lumps will appear. This is due to the egg yolks that are beginning to curdle. To save it, pour into a blender or food processor and briefly blend just to homogenize. Do not blend too long or the custard will liquefy.

Coupe Glacée Rose Framboise

Raspberry Rose Sundae

1 quart | 1 litre rose petal ice cream: see recipe, page 72
1 pint | ½ litre raspberry sorbet: see recipe, page 76
½ cup | 125 ml raspberry coulis: see basic recipe
2 cups | 250 g sweetened whipped cream: see basic recipe
40 to 50 fresh raspberries

Equipment

Piping bag fitted with a star tip
Ice cream scoop

Prepare the ice cream, sorbet and coulis in advance, and the sweetened whipped cream just before serving.

Presentation

In each serving dish, place 2 scoops of rose petal ice cream and 1 scoop of raspberry sorbet.
Top with 5 or 6 raspberries and drizzle with raspberry coulis.
Spoon sweetened whipped cream into the piping bag fitted with a star tip, and pipe a rosette on top.

Chef's tip

The sweetened whipped cream can also be prepared in advance; in this case, keep it in the refrigerator.
You can also fill the dishes with ice cream and sorbet in advance and keep them in the freezer. When ready to serve, all that is left to do is add the raspberries, coulis and sweetened whipped cream.

Makes 1 quart | 1 litre of sorbet *Preparation: 1 hour* *Resting time: 1 hour*

Sorbet Framboise

Raspberry Sorbet

1 ⅔ cups | 400 ml water
1 ¼ cups | 250 g granulated sugar
1 lemon
5 cups | 625 g fresh raspberries

Equipment
Ice cream maker

1 ••• In a saucepan, bring the water and sugar to a boil. Remove from heat and allow to cool.
Juice the lemon.

2 ••• In a blender or food processor, blend the raspberries with the lemon juice until you have a liquid consistency. Stir into the cooled sugar syrup. Strain the mixture through a fine mesh sieve: alternate pressing and scraping with a spoon to obtain as much pulp as possible without the seeds.

3 ••• Pour the preparation into the bowl of an ice cream maker and freeze according to the manufacturer's instructions.
When the sorbet is ready, transfer to an airtight container and store in the freezer at 0°F | -18°C.

Chef's tip
If possible, serve sorbet the same day of preparation, as the texture will be at its best. If you store it in the freezer, simply remove 10 minutes before serving to soften.

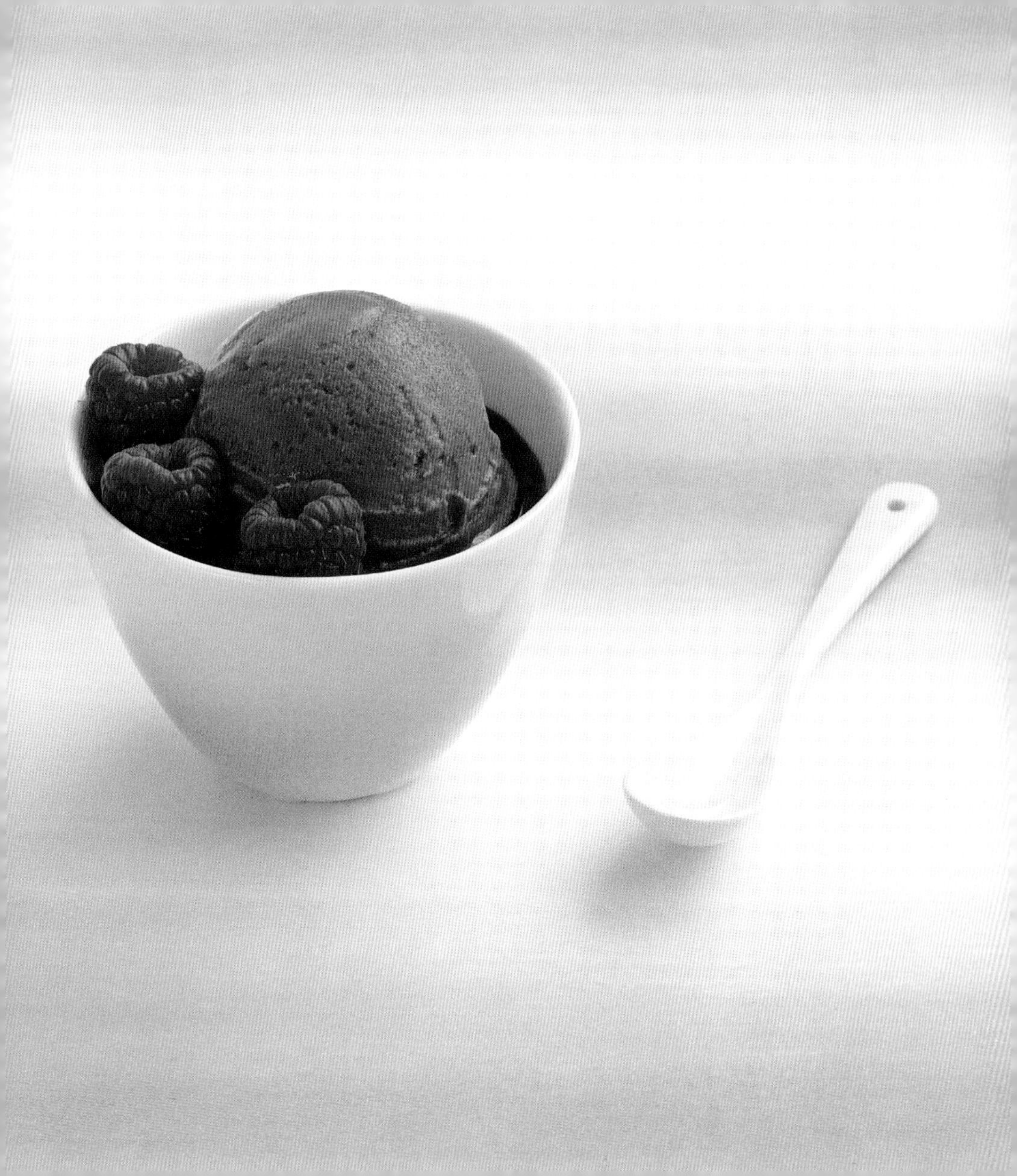

Makes 1 quart | 1 litre of sorbet   Preparation: 1 hour   Resting time: 3 hours

Sorbet Fromage Blanc

Fromage Blanc Sorbet

½ lemon, unwaxed
1 ¼ cups | 300 ml water
1 cup | 200 g granulated sugar
1 cup | 250 g fromage blanc, 40% fat (fresh cheese with a consistency of sour cream or Greek yogurt)

Equipment
Ice cream maker

1 ··· Using a vegetable peeler, remove the zest from the lemon half.
In a saucepan, bring the water, sugar and lemon zest to a boil.
Remove from heat and allow to cool. Cover and allow to infuse for 10 minutes.
Strain syrup with a fine mesh sieve. Discard solids and allow to cool.

2 ··· Juice the lemon half. In a bowl, gradually thin the fromage blanc with the cooled syrup. Incorporate 1 tbsp of lemon juice.
Pour the preparation into the bowl of an ice cream maker and freeze according to the manufacturer's instructions.
When the sorbet is ready, transfer to an airtight container and store in the freezer at 0°F | -18°C.

Chef's tips

Serve sorbet the same day of preparation for the texture to be at its best.
It will keep well for several days in the freezer; simply remove 10 minutes before serving to soften.
This sorbet is a perfect accompaniment to the red berry salad with fresh mint (page 100). It can also be served with fresh red berries (raspberries, strawberries, redcurrants) or just strawberries or raspberries.
You can also top it with a red berry coulis.

For 8 people   Preparation: 15 minutes + basic recipes

Coupe Glacée Chocolat Liégeois

Chocolate Ice Cream Sundae

1 quart | 1 litre dark chocolate ice cream: see recipe, page 82
1 cup | 250 g hot chocolate, cooled: see recipe, page 346
2 cups | 250 g sweetened whipped cream: see basic recipe

⅓ cup | 30 g sliced (flaked) almonds (optional)

Equipment
Piping bag fitted with a star tip
Ice cream scoop

Prepare the dark chocolate ice cream and the hot chocolate in advance (allow the hot chocolate to cool), and the sweetened whipped cream just before serving.

Presentation

Lightly toast the sliced almonds.
In each serving dish, place 2 scoops of chocolate ice cream and coat with 3 spoonfuls of cooled hot chocolate.
Spoon the sweetened whipped cream into the piping bag fitted with a star tip and pipe a rosette on top. Decorate with toasted almonds if desired.

Chef's tip

The sweetened whipped cream can also be prepared in advance; in this case, keep it in the refrigerator. You can also fill the dishes with chocolate ice cream in advance and keep them in the freezer. When ready to serve, all that is left to do is add the hot chocolate, sweetened whipped cream and toasted almonds.

Makes 1 quart | 1 litre of ice cream *Preparation: 1 ½ hours* *Resting time: 3 hours*

Glace au Chocolat Noir

Dark Chocolate Ice Cream

7 oz | 200 g chocolate (minimum 70% cacao solids)
½ cup - 1 tbsp | 100 ml water
2 cups + 2 tbsp | 500 ml whole milk
3 egg yolks
½ cup + 2 tbsp | 120 g granulated sugar

EQUIPMENT
Ice cream maker

1 ••· Using a knife, chop the chocolate on a cutting board.
In a saucepan, bring the water and milk to a boil. Remove from heat.

2 ••· In a large bowl, whisk the egg yolks and sugar until slightly pale. Pour a third of the hot milk over the egg yolks and sugar (to temper the yolks). Stir together with a whisk and pour the whole mixture back into the saucepan.

3 ••· Cook over low heat, stirring constantly with a wooden spoon until the custard thickens. It should coat the spoon when ready; if you run your finger down the back of the spoon, the custard should not run back into the line. Important: the custard should never come to a boil. (It should cook at a maximum of 185°F | 85°C.)

4 ••· As soon as the custard has this consistency, remove from heat and add the chopped chocolate to stop the cooking. Pour into a large bowl and continue to stir for 5 minutes so that the custard stays smooth. Refrigerate until chilled.
Pour the preparation into the bowl of an ice cream maker and freeze according to the manufacturer's instructions.
When the ice cream is ready, transfer to an airtight container and store in the freezer.

Chef's tips

Churn the ice cream 3 hours before serving for the texture to be at its best. It will keep well for several days in the freezer; simply remove 10 minutes before serving to soften.

As in the preparation of pouring custard (crème anglaise): in the 3rd step above, if you let the custard cook a little too long, lumps will appear. This is due to the egg yolks that are beginning to curdle. To save it, pour into a blender or food processor and briefly blend just to homogenize. Do not blend too long or the custard will liquefy.

For 8 people   Preparation: 15 minutes + basic recipes

Coupe Ladurée

Ladurée Sundae

1 quart | 1 litre chestnut ice cream: see recipe, page 86
2 cups | 250 g sweetened whipped cream: see basic recipe
5 ½ oz | 150 g candied chestnuts

Equipment
Piping bag fitted with a ¾-inch | 18-mm star tip
Ice cream scoop

Prepare the chestnut ice cream in advance, and the sweetened whipped cream just before serving.

Presentation

In each serving dish, place 2 scoops of chestnut ice cream. Roughly break apart small pieces of the candied chestnuts and add some to dish. Spoon the sweetened whipped cream into the piping bag fitted with a star tip and pipe a border of rosettes around the edge of the ice cream. Crumble the remaining pieces of candied chestnuts on top.

Chef's tip

The sweetened whipped cream can also be prepared in advance; in this case, keep it in the refrigerator. You can also fill the dishes with ice cream in advance and keep them in the freezer. When ready to serve, all that is left to do is add the candied chestnut pieces and sweetened whipped cream.

Makes 1 quart | 1 litre of ice cream *Preparation: 1 ½ hours* *Resting time: 3 hours*

Glace aux Marrons

Chestnut Ice Cream

2 cups + 2 tbsp | 500 ml whole milk
¾ cup + 1 tbsp | 190 ml heavy (double) cream
6 egg yolks
1 cup | 200 g granulated sugar
8 ½ oz | 240 g unsweetened chestnut puree
1 tbsp dark aged rum (rhum agricole if possible)
3 ½ oz | 100 g candied chestnut pieces

Equipment
Ice cream maker

1 ••• In a saucepan, bring the milk and ½ cup | 125 ml of heavy cream to a boil. Remove from heat.
In a large bowl, whisk the egg yolks and sugar until slightly pale. Pour a third of the hot liquid over the egg yolks and sugar (to temper the yolks). Stir together with a whisk and pour the whole mixture back into the saucepan.

2 ••• Cook over low heat, stirring constantly with a wooden spoon until the custard thickens. It should coat the spoon when ready; if you run your finger down the back of the spoon, the custard should not run back into the line. Important: the custard should never come to a boil. (It should cook at a maximum of 185°F | 85°C.)

3 ••• As soon as the custard has this consistency, remove from heat and add the remaining ¼ cup | 65 ml of heavy cream to stop the cooking.
Place the chestnut puree in a large bowl. Thin the puree by gradually mixing in the custard. Allow to cool and add the rum.

4 ••• Pour the preparation into the bowl of an ice cream maker and freeze according to the manufacturer's instructions.
When the ice cream is ready, pour into a large bowl and add the crumbled candied chestnut pieces. Gently stir together. Transfer to an airtight container and store in the freezer at 0°F | -18°C.

Chef's tips

Churn the ice cream 3 hours before serving for the texture to be at its best. It will keep well for several days in the freezer; simply remove 10 minutes before serving to soften.

As in the preparation of pouring custard (crème anglaise): in the 2nd step above, if you let the custard cook a little too long, lumps will appear. This is due to the egg yolks that are beginning to curdle. To save it, pour into a food processor or blender and briefly blend just to homogenize. Do not blend too long or the custard will liquefy.

For 8 people   *Preparation: 30 minutes*   *Cooking time: 1 hour and 45 minutes*

Ananas Rôti

Roasted Pineapple

1 pineapple
1 vanilla bean
4 tbsp water
+ ¾ cup + 2 tbsp | 200 ml water
½ cup + 2 tbsp | 125 g granulated sugar
1 large orange, juiced (½ cup | 130 ml)
1 tbsp rum

1 ••· Peel the pineapple and slice vertically into 6 equal parts. Remove the core. Place the slices in a baking dish.

2 ••· With a sharp knife, slice the vanilla bean in half lengthwise. Using the tip, scrape the interior to remove the seeds. Pour the 4 tbsp of water into a saucepan and add the vanilla pod and seeds. Bring to a simmer. Remove from heat, cover and allow to infuse for 15 minutes.

3 ••· Preheat the oven to 325°F | 160°C | gas mark 3.
In a large saucepan, cook the sugar and the ¾ cup + 2 tbsp | 200 ml of water. Stir with a wooden spatula to obtain a golden caramel.
Remove from heat, and using caution to avoid burns, stir in the vanilla-infused water (discard the vanilla pod), then the orange juice and rum.

••·

4 ••· Pour this liquid over the pineapple slices. Place in oven and bake for approximately 1 hour and 45 minutes.
Regularly spoon the juices from the baking dish over the pineapple. When it has a deep amber colour, remove from oven and allow to cool completely.

5 ••· Cut the roasted pineapple into small slices approximately ⅕ inch | 5 mm thick.
Arrange pineapple slices in a decorative pattern on individual plates or a serving platter. Serve with passion fruit coulis and vanilla ice cream.

For 8 people *Preparation: 45 minutes* *Resting time: 3 hours*

Nougat Glacé au Miel

Iced Honey Nougat

Iced nougat

1 quart | 1 litre heavy (double) cream, cold
14 oz | 400 g almond nougatine
(caramelized almonds rolled thin)
1 ½ cups | 250 g candied fruit
¼ cup | 30 g shelled raw pistachios
½ cup | 150 g mixed flower honey
8 egg whites

Raspberry coulis

1 cup | 250 ml coulis: see basic recipe

Sweetened whipped cream (see basic recipe) and a handful of raspberries for decoration

EQUIPMENT

8 individual round ring moulds

1 ••• Place a large mixing bowl in the freezer to chill.
Pour the heavy cream into the chilled bowl and whisk energetically until firm. Keep in the refrigerator.
Chop the nougatine and candied fruit into ⅕-inch | 5-mm cubes, and roughly chop the pistachios. Set aside.

2 ••• In a saucepan, cook the honey until it starts to colour slightly (at approximately 250°F | 120°C). Meanwhile, using an electric mixer in a clean, dry bowl, whip the egg whites to a foam.
Once they are firm, add the honey and continue to beat until the mixture has completely cooled down.

•••

3 ••· In a large bowl, delicately fold together the whipped cream and the honey meringue with a rubber spatula. Incorporate the chopped nougatine, candied fruit and pistachios.

4 ••· Fill moulds with preparation and freeze for 3 hours.
Meanwhile, prepare the raspberry coulis and keep in the refrigerator.
Remove the iced nougat from the moulds, place on serving plates and decorate each with a rosette of sweetened whipped cream and a raspberry. Pour raspberry coulis around the dessert.

Chef's tips

If you do not have individual ring moulds, you can use glasses that you put in the freezer.
The iced nougat can also be made in a rectangular mould (about 9 inches | 22 cm long), placed in the freezer for 3 hours. Serve it in slices, drizzled with raspberry coulis.
You can also customize the nougat ingredients by replacing some of the candied fruit (¼ cup | 50 g for example) with cubes of candied orange, ginger or angelica.
This recipe is alcohol-free, but if you would like to add more character, macerate the candied fruit for 1 hour in 3 tbsp (50 ml) of Grand Marnier, and add to the preparation with the other candied fruit above.

For 8 people   Preparation: 45 minutes   Resting time: 2 hours

Minestrone de Fruits Frais au Basilic

Fresh Fruit Minestrone with Basil

Basil syrup

1 lemon, unwaxed

1 orange, unwaxed

1 cup | 250 ml water

¾ cup | 150 g granulated sugar

4 fresh basil leaves

Fruit salad

1 papaya

1 mango

½ large pineapple or 1 small (Victoria) pineapple

3 kiwis

2 passion fruits

3 oranges

2 grapefruits

6 fresh basil leaves

Basil syrup

1 ••• Using a vegetable peeler, remove 2 strips of zest from the lemon and from the orange. In a saucepan, bring the water, sugar and zest to a boil. Chop the basil leaves.

2 ••• Remove from heat and add the chopped basil leaves. Cover and allow to infuse for 30 minutes. Strain the liquid with a fine mesh sieve and discard solids. Set aside.

Fruit salad

3 ••• Peel the papaya, mango, pineapple and kiwis.

•••

4 ••• Prepare each fruit as follows and place in a large salad bowl.
Cut the papaya in half and remove seeds. Divide each half into 4 equal parts, and cut slices ⅓ inch | 8 mm thick.
Slice the mango into two halves, running a knife along both sides of the pit. Divide each half into 3 equal parts lengthwise, and cut slices 1⁄10 inch | 2 mm thick.
Cut the kiwis in half lengthwise. Cut each half again lengthwise into 8 equal parts and then make 4 slices in the opposite direction.
Cut the pineapple in half lengthwise. Cut each half again lengthwise into 4 equal parts. Remove the core and cut into slices ⅛ inch | 3 mm thick.
Slice open the passion fruits and take out the pulp with a spoon.

5 ••• Using a sharp knife, peel the oranges and grapefruits. Separate into segments and remove the white pith and membranes. Add to bowl.

6 ••• Toss all of the fruit together and pour in the basil syrup.
Using a sharp knife, finely chop the remaining 6 basil leaves on a cutting board. Add the basil to the fruit salad and delicately toss together, being careful not to bruise the pieces of fruit. Refrigerate for 2 hours before serving.

Chef's tip

Depending on the season, you can also add strawberries, raspberries and sliced banana just before serving.

Salade de Fruits Rouges Mentholée

Red Berry Salad with Fresh Mint

Red berry syrup with fresh mint

1 ¼ cups | 300 ml water
¾ cup | 150 g granulated sugar
¾ cup | 100 g redcurrants
¾ cup | 100 g raspberries
1 bunch of fresh mint leaves

Fruit

3 ⅓ cups | 500 g strawberries (Gariguette if possible)
1 cup | 125 g redcurrants
2 cups | 250 g raspberries
1 cup | 125 g blackberries
1 cup | 125 g blueberries

Red berry syrup with fresh mint

1 ••• In a saucepan, bring the water, sugar, redcurrants and raspberries to a boil. Remove from heat and add 15 fresh mint leaves. Cover and allow to infuse for 20 minutes.
Remove the mint leaves. Using an immersion hand blender, blend until smooth. Strain the syrup with a fine mesh sieve.

Fruit

2 ••• Wash, hull and slice the strawberries.
Remove redcurrants from stems.

3 ••• Coat plates or fill individual bowls with mint syrup and arrange fruit in a decorative pattern. Keep in the refrigerator until ready to serve.

Chef's tip
Serve this dessert with ice cream, vanilla or verbena for example.

Les Tartes

Tarts & Tartlets

For 8 people *Preparation: 1 hour and 15 minutes + basic recipes*
Cooking time: 45 minutes *Resting time: 2 hours*

Tarte Ananas Rôti

Roasted Pineapple Tart

Roasted pineapple

See recipe, page 88

Coconut cream

5 ½ tbsp | 80 g butter

½ cup | 100 g granulated sugar

¾ cup | 100 g ground coconut (coconut flour)

1 tbsp (10 g) cornstarch (cornflour)

1 egg

1 tbsp rum

1 cup | 250 ml whipping cream

Sweet almond pastry for tart shell

12 ½ oz | 350 g dough: see basic recipe

2 ½ tbsp all-purpose flour for work surface

1 ½ tbsp butter for tart pan

Equipment

Tart pan, 9 ½-inch | 24-cm diameter, ¾ inch | 2 cm high

Prepare the roasted pineapple and sweet almond pastry dough in advance (see basic recipes).

Coconut cream

1 ••• Place a large mixing bowl in the freezer to chill.
Cut the butter into small pieces and put in a heatproof bowl. Place over a pan of gently simmering water or in the microwave to soften, without allowing it to melt. Stir with a spatula until creamy. Add the following ingredients, one after another, making sure to mix well after each addition: sugar, ground coconut, cornstarch, egg and rum.

•••

2 ••• Remove the chilled bowl from the freezer. Pour in the whipping cream and whip energetically.
As soon as it thickens, incorporate into the coconut mixture by gently folding in.

Sweet almond pastry for tart shell

3 ••• Butter the tart pan. On a floured work surface, roll out the dough to the size of the pan, 1/10 inch | 2 mm thick. Refrigerate for 1 hour. Then gently press the dough into the buttered pan. Allow to rest in the refrigerator again for 1 hour.

Filling

4 ••• Preheat the oven to 325°F | 160°C | gas mark 3.
Remove tart shell from the refrigerator. Fill with coconut cream and half of the roasted pineapple slices.
Place in oven and bake for approximately 45 minutes until golden.
Remove from oven, unmould tart and allow to cool.

Chef's tip
Serve tart with a fruit coulis and vanilla ice cream.

Assembly

5 ••• Arrange the remaining roasted pineapple slices in a decorative pattern on the cooled tart.
Keep in the refrigerator until ready to serve.

For 8 people

Preparation: 1 hour and 45 minutes *Cooking time: 40 minutes* *Resting time: 2 hours*

Tarte Tout Chocolat

All Chocolate Tart

Sweet tart dough with cocoa

1 ⅔ cups | 200 g cake flour
+ 2 ½ tbsp cake flour for work surface
½ cup | 120 g butter, very cold
+ 1 tbsp butter for tart pan
⅔ cup | 75 g confectioners' (icing) sugar
¼ cup | 25 g ground almonds (almond flour)
2 ¼ tbsp (12 g) unsweetened cocoa powder
1 pinch of fleur de sel (or other coarse sea salt)
1 egg

Flourless chocolate sponge cake

1 ½ oz | 45 g chocolate (60-70% cacao solids)
3 eggs
⅓ cup | 65 g granulated sugar

Chocolate ganache

10 ½ oz | 300 g chocolate (65-75% cacao solids)
1 ¼ cups | 300 ml whipping cream
7 tbsp | 100 g butter

1 bar of chocolate and cocoa powder for decoration

Equipment

Tart pan, 9 ½-inch | 24-cm diameter, ¾ inch | 2 cm high
Piping bag fitted with a ¼ to ⅓-inch | 7 to 8-mm plain tip

Sweet tart dough with cocoa

I ••• Sift the flour into a large bowl. Cut the chilled butter into very small pieces and add to bowl, along with the confectioners' sugar, ground almonds, cocoa powder and fleur de sel. Using the palms of your hands, work the ingredients together until they resemble fine grain or sand.
When the mixture has this texture, add the egg and combine just until homogenous; do not overwork the dough.
(If you have a stand mixer, you can prepare the dough in the bowl of the mixer fitted with the paddle attachment.)
Form the dough into a ball and wrap in plastic wrap. Refrigerate for a minimum of 1 hour before using. You can also prepare the dough one day ahead; it will be easier to roll out. •••

2 ••• Butter and flour the tart pan. On a floured work surface, roll out the dough to 1⁄10 inch | 2 mm thick, and gently press into the pan. Allow to rest in the refrigerator for 1 hour. Preheat the oven to 340°F | 170°C | gas mark 3. Remove tart shell from the refrigerator. Using a fork, prick the surface of the dough to keep from puffing up during baking. Fit a round piece of parchment paper over the dough, carefully pressing into the corners and working up the sides so it will stay in place in the oven. Place dried beans or pie weights on top, spreading them out in an even layer. Bake for 25 minutes. Take tart shell out of the oven and remove pie weights and parchment paper. Allow to cool.

Flourless chocolate sponge cake

3 ••• Place the chocolate in a heatproof bowl set over a pan of gently simmering water. It should be melted and lukewarm.
Separate the egg whites and egg yolks. In a large bowl, mix the egg yolks with about 3 tbsp (35 g) of sugar and beat until frothy.
In a clean, dry bowl, whip the egg whites to a foam. Once they are frothy, add the remaining 2 tbsp (30 g) of sugar, beating constantly until firm.
Pour ¼ of the whipped egg whites into the egg yolk and sugar mixture. Fold in the melted chocolate. Add the remaining whipped egg whites and gently combine.

4 ••• Preheat the oven to 340°F | 170°C | gas mark 3. Line a baking sheet with parchment paper and transfer chocolate batter to the piping bag fitted with a plain tip. Pipe a disk of batter in a spiral, starting from the center outwards to a diameter ¾ inch | 2 cm smaller than that of the tart shell. Place in oven and bake for approximately 15 minutes. The cake should be baked until slightly dry. Remove from oven and slide the parchment paper onto a cooling rack. Allow to cool.

Chocolate ganache

5 ••• Bring the butter to room temperature.
Using a knife, finely chop the chocolate on a cutting board and place in a large bowl. In a saucepan, bring the cream to a boil. Pour half of the boiling cream over the chocolate in one pour and mix with a whisk in a circular motion to gradually emulsify the mixture. Add the remaining boiled cream and whisk in the same manner.

6 ••• Cut the butter into small pieces and add to the ganache. Using a spatula, stir until smooth. Assemble the tart immediately.

Assembly

7 ••• Pour a thin layer of ganache into the tart shell to a thickness of 1⁄10-1⁄8 inch | 2-3 mm. Place the disk of chocolate sponge cake on top and press down lightly. Fill to the very top with the remaining ganache.
Allow to rest at room temperature for 30 minutes to set.

8 ••• Decorate the top of the tart with chocolate shavings. Scrape the side of the chocolate bar with the back of a knife to make fine shavings. Shave directly over the tart to avoid having to handle the chocolate. Dust lightly with cocoa powder.

For 8 people *Preparation: 1 hour and 15 minutes + basic recipe*
Cooking time: 35 minutes *Resting time: 24 hours*

Tartelettes Citron Vert et Noix de Coco

Lime and Coconut Tartlets

Lime cream

1 lime, unwaxed

¾ cup + 2 tbsp | 170 g granulated sugar

2 tsp (5 g) cornstarch (cornflour)

3 eggs

½ cup | 115 ml lime juice

1 cup + 1 ½ tbsp | 250 g butter, softened

Coconut cream

¼ cup | 60 ml heavy (double) cream, very cold

2 tbsp | 25 g butter, softened

3 tbsp (25 g) confectioners' (icing) sugar

2 tbsp (25 g) shredded coconut

1 tbsp dark rum (rhum agricole if possible)

1 egg

3 tbsp (25 g) cornstarch (cornflour)

Sweet almond pastry for tartlet shells

12 ½ oz | 350 g dough: see basic recipe

3 tbsp all-purpose flour for work surface

1 ½ tbsp butter for tartlet pans

Lime glaze

2 oz | 50 g lime jelly

1 tbsp water

Grated zest of lime and candied lime for decoration

EQUIPMENT

8 tartlet pans, 3-inch | 8-cm diameter, ¾ inch | 2 cm high

Grater

Pastry brush

Prepare the lime cream and sweet almond pastry dough one day ahead.

LIME CREAM

1 ••• Using a grater, zest the lime. In a bowl, mix together the sugar and grated zest. Add the cornstarch, the eggs one at a time, and the lime juice. Pour this mixture into a saucepan and cook over low heat, stirring with a spatula until it simmers, allowing the cream to thicken. Remove from heat. •••

Allow to cool slightly for about 10 minutes. The cream should be hot but not scalding (approximately 140°F | 60°C). Add the softened butter. In a blender or food processor, blend the butter into the cream until the mixture is completely homogenous. Pour into an airtight container and refrigerate for a minimum of 12 hours until firm.

Coconut cream

2 ••• The following day, place a large mixing bowl in the freezer to chill. Pour the cold heavy cream into the chilled bowl and whip energetically until firm. In another bowl, mix the softened butter along with the confectioners' sugar and coconut. Add the rum, egg and cornstarch. Incorporate the whipped cream.

Sweet almond pastry for tartlet shells

3 ••• Butter the tartlet pans. On a floured work surface, roll out the dough to 1⁄10 inch | 2 mm thick. Using a round pastry cutter or small bowl, cut out 8 disks with a diameter of approximately 5 inches | 12 cm and press into buttered pans. Allow to rest in the refrigerator for 1 hour.

4 ••• Preheat the oven to 340°F | 170°C | gas mark 3.
Remove tartlet shells from the refrigerator. Using a fork, prick the surface of the dough to keep from puffing up during baking. Fit a round piece of parchment paper over the dough, carefully pressing into the corners and working up the sides so it will stay in place in the oven. Place dried beans or pie weights on top, spreading them out in an even layer.
Bake for approximately 15 minutes until lightly coloured. Remove tart shells, leaving the oven on.

5 ••· Allow to cool slightly and remove dried beans and parchment paper. Fill with a thin layer of coconut cream (1⁄10-1⁄8 inch | 2-3 mm thick). Return to oven and bake for approximately 10 minutes for the pastry and cream to colour.
Remove from oven, unmould and allow to cool.

6 ••· Spoon the lime cream into the baked tartlet shells, fill to the top of the pastry and smooth the surface with a metal spatula. Freeze to chill the top of the cream (approximately 1 hour).

Lime glaze

7 ••· In a saucepan, stir together the lime jelly and water, and place over low heat. Cook without allowing it to boil (to approximately 122°F to 140°F | 50°C to 60°C) until thick enough to coat the back of a spoon. Remove tartlets from the freezer and using a pastry brush, coat with glaze.
Decorate with grated lime zest, as seen in the photo.

Chef's tips

During berry season, you can use fresh fruit, like strawberries or raspberries, in place of the lime glaze. Red berries are a perfect match with lime and coconut. You can also serve these tartlets with a fruit coulis and mango sorbet or coconut ice cream.
If you do not have lime jelly, you can use lemon jelly or even make your own to use in the recipe.

For 8 people   Preparation: 45 minutes + basic recipes
Cooking time: 1 hour and 5 minutes   Resting time: 1 hour

Tartelettes Croustillantes Abricots ou Cerises

Apricot or Cherry Crumble Tartlets

Shortcrust pastry for tartlet shells
12 ½ oz | 350 g dough: see basic recipe
3 tbsp all-purpose flour for work surface
1 ½ tbsp butter for tartlet pans

Pistachio almond cream
9 oz | 250 g almond cream: see basic recipe
2 tbsp (30 g) pistachio paste
2 tbsp (15 g) shelled raw pistachios
+ 2 tsp (5 g) shelled raw pistachios for decoration

Fruit
about 2 lbs | 1 kg fresh apricots
or 28 oz | 800 g cherries

Crisp sweet pastry for crumble topping
5 ½ oz | 160 g dough: see basic recipe, using 1 ½ oz | 40 g of each ingredient

Confectioners' (icing) sugar for dusting

Equipment
8 tartlet pans, 3-inch | 8-cm diameter, ¾ inch | 2 cm high
Piping bag fitted with a ½-inch | 10-mm plain tip

Prepare the crumble dough in advance.

Shortcrust pastry for tartlet shells

1 ••· Butter the tartlet pans. On a floured work surface, roll out the dough to 1⁄10 inch | 2 mm thick. Using a round pastry cutter or small bowl, cut out 8 disks with a diameter of approximately 5 inches | 12 cm and press into buttered pans. Allow to rest in the refrigerator for 1 hour.

••·

Pistachio almond cream

2 ••· Meanwhile, prepare the almond cream (see basic recipe). Chop pistachios and add to cream, along with the pistachio paste.

3 ••· Preheat the oven to 340°F | 170°C | gas mark 3.
Remove tartlet shells from the refrigerator. Using a fork, prick the surface of the dough to keep from puffing up during baking. Fit a round piece of parchment paper over the dough, carefully pressing into the corners and working up the sides so it will stay in place in the oven. Place dried beans or pie weights on top, spreading them out in an even layer.
Bake for approximately 20 minutes until lightly coloured. Take tartlet shells out of the oven and remove pie weights and parchment paper. Leave the oven on.

Fruit

4 ••· Wash and pit the apricots. Cut in half or in thirds depending on their size. If using cherries, set aside a few whole cherries for decoration. Cut the remaining cherries in half and remove pits.

Filling

5 ••· Transfer the pistachio almond cream to the piping bag fitted with a plain tip. Pipe cream into tartlet shells and arrange apricot slices or pitted cherries in a decorative pattern on top.
Cover with crumble dough, using pieces of various shapes and sizes.

6 ••· Return tartlets to oven and bake for approximately 40 to 45 minutes. Remove from oven and allow to cool. Dust with confectioners' sugar and sprinkle a few crushed pistachios on top.

For 8 people

Preparation: 55 minutes *Cooking time: 20 minutes* *Resting time: 1 ½ hours*

Tarte Fraise Mascarpone

Strawberry Mascarpone Tart

Sweet almond pastry for tart shell

12 ½ oz | 350 g dough: see basic recipe

2 ½ tbsp all-purpose flour for work surface

1 ½ tbsp butter for tart pan

Mascarpone cream

2 gelatin sheets (½ tbsp | 4 g powdered gelatin)

¼ cup | 60 ml heavy (double) cream

½ cup + 2 tbsp | 125 g granulated sugar

2 ¼ cups | 500 g mascarpone

2 ¾ cup | 400 g strawberries

Equipment

Tart pan, 9 ½-inch | 24-cm diameter, ¾ inch | 2 cm high

Sweet almond pastry for tart shell

1 ••• Butter the tart pan. On a floured work surface, roll out the dough to 1⁄10 inch | 2 mm thick and press into the buttered pan. Refrigerate for 1 hour.

2 ••• Preheat the oven to 340°F | 170°C | gas mark 3.

Remove tart shell from the refrigerator. Using a fork, prick the surface of the dough to keep from puffing up during baking. Fit a round piece of parchment paper over the dough, carefully pressing into the corners and working up the sides so it will stay in place in the oven. Place dried beans or pie weights on top, spreading them out in an even layer.

Bake for approximately 20 minutes until lightly coloured. Take out of the oven and remove dried beans and parchment paper. If the pastry is still pale, return to oven uncovered, just long enough to finish baking and to colour slightly. Remove from oven and allow to cool. •••

Mascarpone cream and assembly

3 ••• Place the gelatin sheets in a small bowl of very cold water. Allow to soften for 10 minutes.
Drain the gelatin sheets, squeezing hard to remove all excess liquid.
In a saucepan, bring the cream and sugar to a boil. Remove from heat and incorporate the drained gelatin. Allow to cool completely.

4 ••• Using a wooden or rubber spatula, first mix the mascarpone by itself in a bowl until smooth. Continue to mix and little by little, pour in the cold mixture above.
Fill the cooled baked tart shell with mascarpone cream. Freeze for 20 minutes until the cream is firm.

5 ••• Meanwhile, rinse the strawberries and drain on a dish towel. Hull and slice in half lengthwise. Finish the tart by arranging sliced strawberries in a decorative pattern on top of the cream.

Chef's tip

To make the dough resistant to liquid and prevent it from soaking in the mascarpone cream, brush the baked tart shell with melted white chocolate.
To melt the chocolate: place in a heatproof bowl set over a pan of barely simmering water. Coat pastry and freeze for 10 minutes to harden before filling with cream.

For 8 people

Preparation: 1 hour   *Cooking time: 20 minutes*   *Resting time: minimum of 13 hours*

Tarte Passion Framboise

Raspberry Passion Fruit Tart

Passion fruit cream

1 cup + 1 ½ tbsp | 250 g butter

2 gelatin sheets (½ tbsp | 4 g powdered gelatin)

2 eggs + 1 egg yolk

¾ cup | 150 g granulated sugar

1 tsp cornstarch (cornflour)

⅔ cup | 125 g passion fruit puree

2 tbsp lemon juice

Sweet almond pastry for tart shell

12 ½ oz | 350 g dough: see basic recipe

2 ½ tbsp all-purpose flour for work surface

1 ½ tbsp butter for tart pan

3 ¼ cups | 400 g raspberries

Equipment

Tart pan, 9 ½-inch | 24-cm diameter, ¾ inch | 2 cm high

Passion fruit cream

1 ••• Prepare the cream one day ahead.
Bring the butter to room temperature to soften.
Place the gelatin sheets in a small bowl of very cold water. Allow to soften for 10 minutes.
In a bowl, mix the eggs, egg yolk, sugar and cornstarch. Incorporate the passion fruit puree and lemon juice.
Drain the gelatin sheets, squeezing hard to remove all excess liquid.

2 ••• In a saucepan, cook the egg mixture over low heat, stirring with a spatula until it simmers, allowing the cream to thicken. Remove from heat and incorporate the drained gelatin. •••

Allow to cool slightly for approximately 10 minutes. The cream should be hot but not scalding (less than 140°F | 60°C). Add the softened butter. In a blender or food processor, blend the butter into the cream, until the mixture is homogenous. Pour into an airtight container and refrigerate for a minimum of 12 hours until firm.

Sweet almond pastry for tart shell

3 ••• Butter the tart pan. On a floured work surface, roll out the dough to 1/10 inch | 2 mm thick and press into the buttered pan. Refrigerate for 1 hour. Preheat the oven to 340°F | 170°C | gas mark 3.
Remove tart shell from the refrigerator. Using a fork, prick the surface of the dough to keep from puffing up during baking. Fit a round piece of parchment paper over the dough, carefully pressing into the corners and working up the sides so it will stay in place in the oven. Place dried beans or pie weights on top, spreading them out in an even layer.

Chef's tips
Prepare the tart shell, fill with cream and then keep in the refrigerator. Wait until the last minute to add the fresh raspberries, as they will be more flavourful. This tart is delicious served with raspberry coulis and passion fruit sorbet or vanilla ice cream.

4 ••• Bake for approximately 20 minutes until lightly coloured. Take tart shell out of the oven and remove dried beans and parchment paper. If the pastry is still pale, return to oven uncovered, just long enough to finish baking and to colour slightly. Remove from oven and allow to cool.

Assembly

5 ••• Fill the cooled baked tart shell with passion fruit cream and arrange the raspberries in a decorative pattern on top. Keep in the refrigerator until ready to serve.

For 8 people
Preparation: 1 hour + basic recipe *Cooking time: 40 minutes* *Resting time: 1 hour*

Tartelettes aux Pommes Élysée

Élysée Apple Tartlets

Sweet almond pastry for tartlet shells
12 ½ oz | 350 g dough: see basic recipe
2 ½ tbsp all-purpose flour for work surface
1 ½ tbsp butter for tartlet pans

Diced cinnamon apple
½ cup | 60 g golden seedless raisins (sultanas)
26 ½ oz | 750 g apples (Jonagored, Jonagold or Boskoop if possible)
4 tbsp | 60 g butter
¼ cup | 45 g granulated sugar
1 pinch of ground cinnamon

Baked apple slices
about 2 lbs | 1 kg apples (Jonagold or Boskoop if possible)
4 tbsp | 60 g butter
¼ cup | 50 g granulated sugar

¼ cup | 25 g slivered or sliced (flaked) almonds (optional)

Equipment
8 tartlet pans, 3-inch | 8-cm diameter, ¾ inch | 2 cm high
Pastry brush

Prepare the sweet almond pastry dough one day ahead.

Sweet almond pastry for tartlet shells

1 ••• Butter the tartlet pans. On a floured work surface, roll out the dough to ⅒ inch | 2 mm thick. Using a round pastry cutter or small bowl, cut out 8 disks with a diameter of approximately 5 inches | 12 cm and press into buttered pans. Refrigerate for 1 hour.

Diced cinnamon apple

2 ••• Place raisins in a bowl covered with hot water and allow to soak for approximately 30 minutes.
Meanwhile, peel, core and dice the apples.

•••

Melt the butter in a skillet and add the diced apple to sear, then add the sugar and cinnamon. As soon as the apples are golden, remove from heat. Important: they should be cooked, but still firm. Allow to cool. Drain the raisins and fold in to the apples.

Baked apple slices

3 ••• Preheat the oven to 350°F | 180°C | gas mark 4.
Peel, core and halve the apples. Cut again into either 4 or 5 slices depending on their size. Place on a baking sheet lined with parchment paper.
In a small saucepan (or in the microwave), melt the butter. Using a pastry brush, butter the apple slices. Sprinkle with sugar and bake for 10 to 12 minutes. The apples should remain firm after cooking.

Tartlet shells and assembly

4 ••• Preheat the oven to 340°F | 170°C | gas mark 3.
Remove tartlet shells from the refrigerator. Using a fork, prick the surface of the dough to keep from puffing up during baking. Fit a round piece of parchment paper over the dough, carefully pressing into the corners and working up the sides so it will stay in place in the oven. Place dried beans or pie weights on top, spreading them out in an even layer.
Bake for approximately 20 minutes until lightly coloured.

Take tartlet shells out of the oven and remove dried beans and parchment paper. Allow to cool. If the pastry is still pale, return to oven uncovered, just long enough to finish baking and to colour slightly. Remove from oven and allow to cool.

5 ••• Fill the cooled tartlet shells with the diced cinnamon apple and arrange the baked apple slices in a decorative pattern on top. Keep in the refrigerator until ready to serve.
Sprinkle with toasted almonds if desired.

Chef's tip

If you would like to give tartlets a glossy sheen, you can coat the apple slices with apricot glaze.

Makes 8 individual tartlets
Preparation: 1 hour and 10 minutes *Cooking time: 20 minutes* *Resting time: 12 hours*

Tartelettes Rhubarbe et Fraises des Bois

Rhubarb & Wild Strawberry Tartlets

Sweet almond pastry for tartlet shells
12 ½ oz | 350 g dough: see basic recipe
2 ½ tbsp all-purpose flour for work surface
1 ½ tbsp butter for tartlet pans

Rhubarb compote
21 oz | 600 g rhubarb
¼ cup | 45 g granulated sugar
+ ⅓ cup | 60 g granulated sugar
2 tbsp (18 g) pectin (powder)
6 gelatin sheets (1 ½ tbsp | 11 g powdered gelatin)
½ cup | 120 ml water

12 ½ oz | 350 g wild strawberries (fraises des bois if possible)

Equipment
8 tartlet pans, 3 to 3 ½-inch | 8 to 9-cm diameter, ¾ inch | 2 cm high

Prepare the sweet almond pastry dough and rhubarb compote one day ahead.

Rhubarb compote

1 ••• Using a small knife, peel the rhubarb, pulling off strings. Roughly chop.
In a bowl, mix the ¼ cup | 45 g of sugar with the pectin.
Place the gelatin sheets in a bowl of very cold water. Allow to soften for 10 minutes. Drain well, squeezing hard to remove all excess liquid, and set aside.

•••

2 ••• In a saucepan, heat the ½ cup | 120 ml of water to lukewarm. Dissolve the sugar and pectin mixture in the water. Bring to a boil and while stirring constantly, add the chopped rhubarb. Cook for 4 to 5 minutes, just long enough for the rhubarb to break down. When completely soft, add the remaining sugar and stir gently. Remove from heat and incorporate the softened, drained gelatin.

3 ••• Transfer the rhubarb compote to a rectangular baking dish and spread out in a thin, even layer. Allow to cool completely, then cover with plastic wrap and refrigerate for 12 hours.

Sweet almond pastry for tartlet shells

4 ••• The following day, preheat the oven to 340°F | 170°C | gas mark 3. Butter the tartlet pans. On a floured work surface, roll out the dough to ¹⁄₁₀ inch | 2 mm thick. Using a round pastry cutter or small bowl, cut out 8 disks with a diameter of approximately 5 inches | 12 cm and press into buttered pans. Place in oven and bake for approximately 20 minutes until lightly coloured. Allow to cool.

5 ••• Fill the tartlet shells with the jellied rhubarb compote. Arrange wild strawberries in a decorative pattern on each tartlet. Keep in the refrigerator until ready to serve.

Variations

You can replace the wild strawberries with other strawberry varieties, like Gariguette or Mara des Bois, for example.
In the absence of red berries, these tartlets are also excellent topped with baked apple slices (see Élysée Apple Tartlets, page 128).

Chef's tip

Remove tartlets from the refrigerator 20 minutes before serving so that the strawberries come to room temperature and will thus be more fragrant.

Makes 8 individual tarts

Preparation: 45 minutes *Cooking time: 2 hours and 15 minutes* *Resting time: 3 hours*

Tartes Tatin

Upside-Down Apple Tarts

Tatin apples

12 apples (Golden if possible)

Caramel

½ cup - 1 tbsp | 100 ml water

1 ½ cups | 300 g granulated sugar

9 tbsp | 125 g butter

Puff pastry top

17 ½ | 500 g dough: see basic recipe

2 ½ tbsp all-purpose flour for work surface

EQUIPMENT

8 ramekins, 4-inch | 10-cm diameter

Round pastry cutter, 5-inch | 13-cm diameter

TATIN APPLES AND CARAMEL

1 ••• Peel, core and cut apples into 3 large slices. Cut the butter into pieces. In a saucepan, cook the sugar and water together until the mixture has a golden caramel colour.
Remove from heat and immediately add the butter to stop the cooking, being careful not to burn yourself. Stand back and stir until homogenous.
Pour the caramel into the ramekins to a thickness of ⅕ inch | 5 mm.
Allow to cool.

2 ••• Preheat the oven to 325°F | 160°C | gas mark 3.
Fit the apple slices into the ramekins as tightly as possible, upright and side by side. The apples should be higher than the ramekin; they will shrink in half during baking. Place in oven and bake for 1 ½ hours.
Remove from oven and allow to cool.

•••

Puff pastry top

3 ••• On a floured work surface, roll out the puff pastry dough. Using a round pastry cutter, cut out 5-inch | 13-cm diameter disks and allow them to rest in the refrigerator for 30 minutes.
Preheat the oven to 340°F | 170°C | gas mark 3.

4 ••• Cover the apples with the rounds of pastry and push down around the interior of the ramekins to encase the fruit and make sure it stays in place when removing from the mould. Place in oven and bake for 35 minutes. Allow to cool, then refrigerate for a minimum of 2 hours for the caramel to set and for the pectin in the apples to jellify.

5 ••• Heat water in a sauteuse pan. Dip the bottoms of the ramekins one by one into the hot water for 15 seconds (to slightly soften the hardened caramel). Run the blade of a knife around the interior of each ramekin to loosen the tarts. Press down lightly on the pastry to push the tart up and unmould on a serving plate, apples facing up.

Chef's tip

When ready to serve, reheat tarts at 250°F | 120°C | gas mark ½ and serve lukewarm with whipped cream.
You can also serve with a scoop of vanilla ice cream. The contrast of hot and cold gives a very enjoyable sensation.

Les Entremets et Verrines

Custards, Crèmes & Puddings

For 6 people
Preparation: 15 minutes   *Cooking time: 1 hour*   *Resting time: 2 hours*

Crème Brûlée à la Fleur d'Oranger

Orange Flower Crème Brûlée

¾ cup + 1 tbsp | 200 ml whole milk
1 cup + 1 tbsp | 250 ml heavy (double) cream
6 egg yolks
½ cup - ½ tbsp | 85 g granulated sugar
3 ⅓ tbsp (50 ml) orange flower water
about ¼ cup | 50 g brown sugar for finish

Equipment
Crème brûlée moulds, 3 to 4-inch | 8 to 10-cm diameter, ¾ to 1 ¼ inches | 2 to 3 cm high

1 ••• In a saucepan, bring the milk and cream to a boil.
In a large bowl, whisk the egg yolks and sugar until pale. Gradually add the milk and cream mixture and the orange flower water.

2 ••• Preheat the oven to 210°F | 100°C | gas mark ¼.
Pour preparation into moulds. Put them in a roasting pan or on a high-rimmed baking sheet. Place in oven and pour water into pan or onto sheet, to ⅕ inch | 5 mm below the rim of the moulds. Bake (in a bain-marie) for 1 hour.
The custard is cooked when it is softly set. Check to see if it is done by inserting the tip of a knife; it should still jiggle slightly in the center.

•••

3 ••• Remove moulds from oven and allow to cool completely. Cover with plastic wrap to prevent moisture from collecting on the surface, and refrigerate for a minimum of 2 hours.

4 ••• When ready to serve, preheat the oven to the broil setting. Meanwhile, remove custards from the refrigerator and sprinkle the tops evenly with brown sugar. Place in oven and caramelize for 2 minutes under the broiler, keeping a close eye that they do not darken too much. When the sugar has a deep caramel colour, remove from oven and serve immediately.

Variation

Vanilla crème brûlée: remove the orange flower water and instead, add 5 tbsp of whole milk. With a sharp knife, slice 2 vanilla beans in half lengthwise. Using the tip, scrape the interior to remove the seeds. Pour the milk and cream into a saucepan and add the vanilla pods and seeds. Bring to a boil. Remove from heat, cover and allow to infuse for 15 minutes. Remove the vanilla pods and continue with step 2.

Makes 8 ramekins *Preparation: 20 minutes* *Cooking time: 1 hour*

Crème Renversée au Caramel

Crème Caramel

Custard

2 vanilla beans

2 ½ cups | 600 ml whole milk

1 ⅔ cups | 400 ml heavy (double) cream

4 eggs + 4 egg yolks

1 cup | 200 g granulated sugar

Caramel

10 tbsp water

+ 3 tbsp water, hot

1 ¼ cups | 250 g granulated sugar

EQUIPMENT

8 ramekins

1 ••• With a sharp knife, slice the vanilla beans in half lengthwise. Using the tip, scrape the interior to remove the seeds. Pour the milk and cream into a saucepan and add the vanilla pods and seeds. Bring to a simmer. Remove from heat, cover and allow to infuse for 15 minutes.

2 ••• Meanwhile, cook the 10 tbsp of water and the sugar in a saucepan until the mixture has a golden caramel colour.

Remove from heat and dip the bottom of the pan in cold water to stop the cooking. Immediately add the 3 tbsp of hot water, being very careful not to burn yourself. Standing back, stir the water and caramel together until homogenous. If the caramel thickens too much on the bottom of the saucepan, put back over low heat for 30 seconds and stir with a wooden spatula until homogenous. Pour the caramel into the ramekins to a thickness of ⅛ to ⅙ inch | 3 to 4 mm. Allow to cool completely.

•••

3 ••• In a large bowl, whip the eggs, egg yolks and sugar until slightly pale. Remove the vanilla pods from the milk and cream mixture, and reheat. Pour a third of this hot liquid over the egg mixture (to temper the yolks), gently whisking together without making it frothy. Add the remaining ⅔ of liquid.

4 ••• Preheat the oven to 340°F | 170°C | gas mark 3.
Pour the custard into the ramekins, filling to about ⅛ inch | 2 or 3 mm below the rim.
Put ramekins in a roasting pan. Place in oven and pour water into pan to ⅕ inch | 5 mm below the rim of the ramekins. Bake (in a bain-marie) for 1 hour.

5 ••• Remove from oven, allow to cool completely and keep in the refrigerator until ready to serve.
To remove from the ramekins, delicately slide a knife around the inside of the ramekin. Turn upside down onto serving plates.

Makes 8 custard cups
Preparation: 15 minutes   *Cooking time: 1 hour*   *Resting time: 2 hours*

Petits Pots de Crème à la Rose

Rose-Flavoured Baked Custards

¾ cup + 1 tbsp | 200 ml whole milk
1 cup + 1 tbsp | 250 ml heavy (double) cream
6 egg yolks
½ cup - ½ tbsp | 85 g granulated sugar
4 tbsp rose syrup
3 drops of natural rose essential oil
3 tbsp rose water

EQUIPMENT

8 custard cups, ¼ cup | 2 oz | 60 ml (espresso cups can also be used)

1 ••• In a saucepan, bring the milk and cream to a boil.
In a large bowl, whisk the egg yolks and sugar until pale. Gradually add the milk and cream mixture, then the syrup, essential oil and rose water.

2 ••• Preheat the oven to 210°F | 100°C | gas mark ¼.
Pour the rose custard into the cups and put in a roasting pan or on a high-rimmed baking sheet. Place in oven and pour water into pan or onto sheet to ⅕ inch | 5 mm below the rim of the cups. (You can cover the pan with plastic wrap, although it is not necessary.) Bake (in a bain-marie) for 1 hour.
The custard is cooked when it is softly set. Check to see if it is done by inserting the tip of a knife; it should still jiggle slightly in the center.

3 ••• Remove from oven and allow to cool completely. Cover with plastic wrap to prevent moisture from collecting on the surface, and refrigerate for a minimum of 2 hours before serving.

For 8 people   Preparation: 1 hour + basic recipe   Cooking time: 4 minutes

Oeufs à la Neige

"Eggs in the Snow"

Oeufs à la neige

1 quart | 1 litre whole milk (will also be used for pouring custard)

10 egg whites

½ cup | 100 g granulated sugar

Pouring custard (crème anglaise)

4 cups | 1 litre pouring custard: see basic recipe, prepared with milk used to cook egg whites

Caramel

½ cup - 1 tbsp | 100 ml water

2 cups | 400 g granulated sugar

Oeufs à la neige

1 ••• In a large deep sauté pan, bring milk to a simmer over low heat, without allowing it to boil.

2 ••• Meanwhile, in a large clean, dry bowl, whip 5 egg whites to a foam. Once they are white and frothy, add ¼ cup | 50 g of sugar and continue to whip until firm. Using 2 spoons dipped in water, form large quenelles (3-sided ovals) of whipped egg white. Slide each into the pan by dipping the spoon in the hot milk, thus detaching the egg whites from the spoon. Form quenelles with all of the whipped egg white and turn off heat. The milk must absolutely not boil, or else the egg whites will deflate and will then resemble fried eggs. Cook for 2 minutes, turn over and cook for another 2 minutes.

Using a skimmer (or slotted spoon), drain the cooked egg whites and place on a damp dish towel. •••

3 ••• Reheat the milk and bring to a simmer. Repeat step 2 with the remaining 5 egg whites and ¼ cup | 50 g of sugar.

Pouring custard

4 ••• Strain the milk used above and measure 2 cups + 2 tbsp | 500 ml. Prepare the pouring custard according to the basic recipe. Allow to cool.

Caramel

5 ••• In a saucepan, cook the water and sugar together until the mixture has a golden caramel colour.
Remove from heat and immediately dip the bottom of the saucepan in cold water for 30 seconds to stop the cooking.
Remove from water and stir with a spoon to homogenize the caramel.
Coat the egg whites with caramel, being careful not to burn yourself.
If the caramel is too liquid, slightly cool it once again by dipping the bottom of the saucepan in cold water.

6 ••• Pour the custard (at room temperature) into a serving dish or individual plates. Carefully place the egg whites coated in caramel on top.

Chef's tip
Serve the pouring custard at room temperature, and pour the caramel over the egg whites 1 to 2 hours before serving so that the caramel starts to lightly melt onto the egg whites. The layer of caramel will be thinner and more enjoyable when tasting.

For 8 people Preparation: 30 minutes Resting time: 4 hours

Mousse au Chocolat

Chocolate Mousse

11 oz | 320 g dark chocolate (70% cacao solids)
5 ½ tbsp | 80 g butter
8 eggs
1 pinch of salt
½ cup - 1 tbsp | 80 g granulated sugar

1 bar of chocolate for decoration

Equipment

Piping bag fitted with a ¾-inch | 18-mm star tip

Chocolate Mousse

1 ••• Using a knife, chop the chocolate on a cutting board and place in a large heatproof bowl. Cut the butter into small pieces and add to bowl. Place over a pan of gently simmering water and melt the chocolate and butter, stirring together.
When the mixture has melted, remove from heat and allow to cool to barely lukewarm (64°F to 68°F | 18°C to 20°C).

2 ••• Separate the egg yolks from the egg whites and place in a bowl. Set egg whites aside.

3 ••• Lightly beat the egg yolks to liquefy.
Place the egg whites in a large clean, dry bowl with a pinch of salt. Whip to a foam. Once they are white and frothy, add the sugar and continue to whip until firm.

•••

Immediately add the egg yolks, incorporating delicately with a whisk, but do not whisk: simply start with the whisk in the center of the bowl, work up the sides of the bowl and bring back down towards the center, all the while turning the bowl regularly. This will result in a smooth and homogenous mixture.

4 ••· Incorporate ¼ of the egg mixture into the butter and chocolate, by gently folding in with a rubber spatula. Pour this entire mixture back over the remaining ¾ of the eggs, always mixing gently, by starting with the spatula in the center of the bowl, working up the sides and bringing the preparation back down towards the center.

Presentation

5 ••· Transfer the chocolate mousse to a large serving dish. Refrigerate for 3 to 4 hours and top with chocolate shavings by scraping the side of a chocolate bar with the back of a small knife (see recipe for the All Chocolate Tart, step 8, page 111).
For individual servings, allow the mousse to become slightly firm in the refrigerator for approximately 15 minutes. Transfer to the piping bag fitted with a star tip and pipe mousse into ramekins, forming a rosette on top.

For 6 to 8 people

Preparation: 50 minutes *Cooking time: 25 minutes* *Resting time: 1 hour*

Riz au Lait

Rice Pudding

½ cup | 60 g golden seedless raisins (sultanas)
¼ cup | 50 g Italian round short-grain rice (Arborio if possible)
2 ½ cups | 600 ml whole milk, cold
1 pinch of fleur de sel (or other coarse sea salt)
2 ⅔ tbsp | 35 g granulated sugar
2 egg yolks
2 tbsp | 30 g butter

1 ••• Soak the raisins in a bowl of hot water.
Rinse the rice in cold water. Bring a saucepan of water to a boil and cook rice for 1 minute, then drain.

2 ••• In another saucepan, bring the milk and salt to a boil. Add the rice and sugar. Cook over low heat for approximately 20 minutes until the rice has absorbed a large portion of the liquid. Remove from heat.

3 ••• Place the egg yolks in a large bowl.
Pour ¼ of the rice preparation over the egg yolks, mixing vigorously. Pour the entire mixture back into the saucepan.
Drain the softened raisins and add to the saucepan, along with the butter. Stir to combine. Return saucepan over heat, stirring gently so that the mixture does not stick to the pan. As soon as it reaches a boil, remove from heat.

4 ••• Pour the rice pudding into a large baking dish. Cover with plastic wrap to prevent it from forming a crust and from drying out while it cools down. Once cool, refrigerate for a minimum of 1 hour. Fill serving dishes with rice pudding. Serve cold.

Chef's tip
The rice puddings can be prepared one day ahead.

Makes 8 verrines

Preparation: 3 hours + basic recipe *Cooking time: 20 minutes* *Resting time: 1 hour*

Verrines Rose Framboise

Raspberry Rose Verrines

Ladyfingers

See basic recipe, prepared with:

3 tbsp (25 g) all-purpose flour

2 ½ tbsp (25 g) potato starch

3 eggs

⅓ cup + 1 tbsp | 75 g granulated sugar

2 ½ tbsp (20 g) confectioners' (icing) sugar

Rose Bavarian cream

4 gelatin sheets (1 tbsp | 7 g powdered gelatin)

3 egg yolks

2 ½ tbsp (30 g) granulated sugar

1 cup + 1 tbsp | 250 ml whole milk

3 tbsp rose water

4 tbsp rose syrup

3 drops natural rose essential oil

1 ½ cups | 350 ml heavy (double) cream, very cold

Rose-flavoured syrup

½ cup - 1 tbsp | 100 ml water

2 tbsp rose water

½ cup + 2 tbsp | 125 g granulated sugar

2 tbsp rose syrup

Jellied raspberry coulis

4 gelatin sheets (1 tbsp | 7 g powdered gelatin)

6 cups | 750 g raspberries

⅓ cup | 70 g granulated sugar

2 tbsp lemon juice

3 tbsp water

32 raspberries for assembly

1 rose and 8 raspberries for decoration

Equipment

8 verrines, ¼ cup | 6 oz | 180 ml (2 ¾-inch | 7-cm diameter, 2 ¾ inches | 7 cm high)

Ladyfingers

1 ••• In advance, prepare the ladyfinger batter and bake 16 disks (2 per verrine) with a diameter ⅖ inch | 1 cm less than that of the verrines.

•••

Rose Bavarian cream

2 ••• Place the gelatin sheets in a small bowl of very cold water. Allow to soften for 10 minutes.
In a large bowl, whisk the egg yolks and sugar until slightly pale.
Drain the gelatin sheets, squeezing hard to remove all excess liquid.

3 ••• In a saucepan, bring the milk, rose water and rose syrup to a simmer. Pour a third of this hot liquid over the egg yolks and sugar (to temper the yolks). Whisk together and pour the entire mixture back into the saucepan. Cook over low heat, stirring constantly with a wooden spoon until the custard thickens. It should coat the spoon when ready; if you run your finger down the back of the spoon, the custard should not run back into the line. Important: the custard should never come to a boil. (It should cook at a maximum of 185°F | 85°C.)
As soon as it has this consistency, remove from heat, add the drained gelatin to stop the cooking and pour into a large bowl. Continue to stir for 5 minutes so that the Bavarian cream stays smooth. Allow to cool completely and add the drops of rose essential oil.

Rose-flavoured syrup

4 ••• Put the water, rose water and sugar in a saucepan and bring to a boil. Remove from heat and add the rose syrup. Allow to cool.

Jellied raspberry coulis

5 ••• Place a large mixing bowl in the freezer to chill.
Put the gelatin sheets in a small bowl of very cold water. Allow to soften for 10 minutes.
Using an immersion hand blender or food processor, blend the raspberries with the sugar until you have a liquid consistency. Strain the mixture through a fine mesh sieve; alternate pressing and scraping with a spoon to obtain as much pulp as possible without the raspberry seeds. To make this easier, just before all of the raspberry puree has been strained, add the lemon juice and water to the sieve, which will pass through with any remaining raspberry pulp.

6 ••• In a saucepan, heat ¼ of this preparation to lukewarm. Drain the gelatin sheets, squeezing hard to remove all excess liquid. Add gelatin to the saucepan and stir to melt. Pour this mixture over the remaining ¾ cold raspberry pulp. Mix together and pour a first layer of coulis into the verrines. Place in the freezer to set.

•••

Final steps for Bavarian cream and assembly

7 ••• Remove the bowl from the freezer and pour in the chilled heavy cream. Whisk energetically until it thickens and becomes firm.
Whisk the rose Bavarian cream, barely set, until smooth. Gently fold in the whipped cream with a rubber spatula. Keep at room temperature.

8 ••• Remove the verrines from the freezer. Lightly soak the ladyfinger disks in the rose-flavoured syrup and place on the jellied coulis already in the verrines. Place 4 raspberry halves in each verrine and cover with Bavarian cream. Freeze until set (approximately 10 minutes).
Repeat previous steps: jellied coulis, ladyfinger disk (soaked in syrup), raspberry halves and Bavarian cream.
When the second layer of Bavarian cream is set, cover with a thin layer of coulis.
Decorate each verrine with a rose petal and a raspberry.

Makes 8 verrines

Preparation: 3 hours *Cooking time: 20 minutes* *Resting time: 1 hour*

Verrines Passion Noix de Coco

Coconut Passion Fruit Verrines

Coconut sponge cake

½ cup - 1 tbsp | 40 g ground almonds (almond flour)

⅔ cup | 80 g confectioners' (icing) sugar

¼ cup | 40 g ground coconut (coconut flour)

3 egg whites

2 ½ tbsp (30 g) granulated sugar

Jellied passion fruit coulis

3 gelatin sheets (¾ tbsp | 5 g powdered gelatin)

1 ½ cups + 2 tbsp | 400 ml passion fruit juice

Passion fruit cream

2 ½ gelatin sheets (⅔ tbsp | 4 g powdered gelatin)

⅓ cup | 60 g granulated sugar

3 tbsp (25 g) cornstarch (cornflour)

1 ⅓ cups | 320 ml heavy (double) cream

1 ¼ cups | 300 ml passion fruit juice

Coconut gelée

3 gelatin sheets (¾ tbsp | 5 g powdered gelatin)

¾ cup + 1 tbsp | 200 ml whole milk, cold

⅓ cup | 50 g ground coconut (coconut flour)

5 oz | 150 g coconut pulp

Equipment

8 verrines, ¼ cup | 6 oz | 180 ml (2 ¾-inch | 7-cm diameter, 2 ¾ inches | 7 cm high)

Piping bag fitted with a ½-inch | 10-mm plain tip

Coconut sponge cake

1 ••• In a large bowl, mix the ground almonds, confectioners' sugar and ground coconut.

In a clean, dry bowl, whip the egg whites to a foam. Once they are frothy, add the granulated sugar and continue to whip until sugar is dissolved.

Using a rubber spatula, gently fold the dry coconut mixture into the whipped egg whites.

•••

2 ••• Preheat the oven to 340°F | 170°C | gas mark 3.
Transfer batter to the piping bag fitted with a plain tip. On a baking sheet lined with parchment paper, pipe 16 disks (2 per verrine) with a diameter ⅖ inch | 1 cm less than that of the verrines. Place in oven and bake for 15 minutes. Allow to cool.

Jellied passion fruit coulis

3 ••• Place the gelatin sheets in a small bowl of very cold water. Allow to soften for 10 minutes.
In a saucepan, heat about ¼ cup | 80 ml of passion fruit juice to lukewarm. Drain the gelatin sheets, squeezing hard to remove all excess liquid. Add to the saucepan and stir to melt. Pour this mixture over the remaining cold passion fruit juice. Combine and immediately pour a first layer of coulis into the verrines. Place in the freezer to set.

Passion fruit cream

4 ••• Place the gelatin sheets in a small bowl of very cold water. Allow to soften for 10 minutes.
Place a large mixing bowl in the freezer to chill.
In another large bowl, mix the sugar and cornstarch and add ⅙ cup | 50 ml of heavy cream.
In a saucepan, bring the passion fruit juice and ½ cup | 120 ml of heavy cream to a simmer.
Pour a portion of this hot liquid over the sugar, cornstarch and cream

mixture, and then pour the entire mixture back into the saucepan. Bring to a boil while stirring constantly with a whisk. Transfer this passion fruit cream to a bowl.
Drain the gelatin sheets, squeezing hard to remove all excess liquid. Add to the hot cream and stir to melt. Allow to cool.

5 ••• Remove the mixing bowl from the freezer. Pour in the remaining ⅔ cup | 150 ml of heavy cream (very cold) and whisk energetically until it thickens and becomes firm.
Whisk the passion fruit cream until smooth and gently fold in the whipped cream with a rubber spatula.

Coconut gelée

6 ••• Place the gelatin sheets in a small bowl of very cold water. Allow to soften for 10 minutes. In a saucepan, bring the milk to a simmer. Pour in the ground coconut and stir to combine.
Drain the gelatin sheets, squeezing hard to remove all excess liquid. Stir gelatin into the hot milk and coconut. Allow to cool to room temperature (64°F | 18°C), then add the coconut pulp. Mix together and keep at room temperature.

•••

Assembly

7 ••• Remove the verrines from the freezer. Place a disk of coconut cake on top of the jellied coulis already in the verrines. Cover with a layer of passion fruit cream. Freeze until set.

Cover cream with a layer of coconut gelée and freeze again to set.

Add a layer of passion fruit cream and then another of coconut gelée; once again passion fruit cream then coconut gelée. Place a second disk of coconut cake, and cover with passion fruit cream.

Allow each layer to set in the freezer and top the verrine with a final layer of jellied coulis. Keep in the refrigerator until ready to serve.

Chef's tip

Serve verrines with a small exotic fruit salad and/or a coconut tuile.

Makes 8 verrines *Preparation: 3 hours* *Cooking time: 15 minutes* *Resting time: 1 hour*

Verrines Pistache Griottes

Pistachio Sour Cherry Verrines

Pistachio dacquoise (meringue)

2 tsp (10 g) pistachio paste
¾ cup | 70 g ground almonds (almond flour)
⅔ cup | 80 g confectioners' (icing) sugar
2 tbsp (15 g) shelled raw pistachios
3 egg whites
2 ½ tbsp (30 g) granulated sugar

Pistachio Bavarian cream

3 gelatin sheets (¾ tbsp | 5 g powdered gelatin)
3 egg yolks
2 ⅔ tbsp (35 g) granulated sugar
2 ½ tbsp (40 g) pistachio paste
1 cup + 1 tbsp | 250 ml whole milk
1 cup + 2 tbsp | 280 ml heavy (double) cream, very cold
2 tsp kirsch liqueur

Cherry confit

3 gelatin sheets (¾ tbsp | 5 g powdered gelatin)
½ cup | 100 g granulated sugar
2 ⅓ tbsp (20 g) pectin (powder)
⅓ cup | 70 ml water
24 ½ oz | 700 g pitted Morello cherries
(or other sour cherry)

Crisp sweet pastry for crumble

10 ½ oz | 300 g pastry: see basic recipe

EQUIPMENT

8 verrines, ¼ cup | 6 oz | 180 ml (2 ¾-inch | 7-cm diameter, 2 ¾ inches | 7 cm high)
Piping bag fitted with a ½-inch | 10-mm plain tip

PISTACHIO DACQUOISE

1 ••• Place the pistachio paste in a bowl.
Combine the ground almonds, confectioners' sugar and the pistachios in a food processor and pulse to obtain a fine powder.
Preheat the oven to 340°F | 170°C | gas mark 3.
In a clean, dry bowl, whip the egg whites to a foam. Once they are frothy, add the granulated sugar and whip until sugar is dissolved.

•••

2 ••• Thin the pistachio paste by mixing in a portion of the whipped egg whites. Pour this mixture back into the remaining egg whites. Using a rubber spatula, gently fold in the ground pistachio mixture.
Transfer this preparation to the piping bag fitted with a plain tip. On a baking sheet lined with parchment paper, pipe 16 disks (2 per verrine) with a diameter ⅖ inch | 1 cm less than that of the verrines.
Place in oven and bake for 15 minutes. Allow to cool.

Pistachio Bavarian cream

3 ••• Place the gelatin sheets in a small bowl of very cold water. Allow to soften for 10 minutes.
Place a large mixing bowl in the freezer to chill.
In another large bowl, whisk the egg yolks and sugar until slightly pale, then add the pistachio paste.
Drain the gelatin sheets, squeezing hard to remove all excess liquid.

4 ••• In a saucepan, bring the milk to a simmer. Pour a third of the hot milk over the egg yolk, sugar and pistachio mixture (to temper the yolks). Whisk together and pour the whole mixture back into the saucepan. Cook over low heat, stirring constantly with a wooden spoon until the custard thickens. It should coat the spoon when ready; if you run your finger down the back of the spoon, the custard should not run back into the line. Important: the custard should never come to a boil. (It should cook at a maximum of 185°F | 85°C.)
As soon as it has this consistency, remove from heat, add the drained gelatin to stop the cooking and pour into a large bowl. Continue to stir for 5 minutes so that the Bavarian cream stays smooth. Allow to cool.

Cherry confit

5 ••• Place the gelatin sheets in a small bowl of very cold water. Allow to soften for 10 minutes.

Mix the sugar and pectin in a bowl. In a saucepan, heat the water to lukewarm and add the sugar and pectin mixture. Bring to a simmer and add the cherries. Cook over low heat for 5 minutes. Remove from heat and incorporate the drained gelatin sheets. Transfer to a baking dish to cool for approximately 10 minutes.

Assembly and final steps for Bavarian cream

6 ••• Place a first layer of cherry confit in the verrines. Freeze to set.

Meanwhile, remove the bowl from the freezer and pour in the chilled heavy cream. Whisk energetically until it thickens and becomes firm.

Whisk the cooled pistachio Bavarian cream until smooth, and add the kirsch. Gently fold in the whipped cream with a rubber spatula. Keep at room temperature.

7 ••• Remove the verrines from the freezer and place a disk of pistachio dacquoise on top of the cherry confit. Cover with pistachio Bavarian cream. Freeze to set (approximately 10 minutes).

Place the second layer of confit and freeze for another 10 minutes.

Place the second layer of dacquoise, cover with Bavarian cream and allow to set again.

Decorate each verrine with the baked crumble topping.

Makes 8 verrines *Preparation: 30 minutes + basic recipes* *Cooking time: 2 hours*

Verrines Mont-Blanc

Mont-Blanc Verrines

Meringue

See recipe, page 338

Chestnut vermicelli

7 oz | 200 g unsweetened chestnut paste
2 tbsp rum
14 oz | 400 g unsweetened chestnut puree
7 oz | 200 g chestnut cream

Sweetened whipped cream

4 cups | 500 g sweetened whipped cream: see basic recipe

8 candied chestnut halves for decoration

EQUIPMENT

8 verrines, ¼ cup | 6 oz | 180 ml (2 ¾-inch | 7-cm diameter, 2 ¾ inches | 7 cm high)
Piping bag fitted with a ½-inch | 14-mm plain tip
Piping bag fitted with a vermicelli tip or a ⅖-inch | 10-mm plain tip

MERINGUE

1 ••• Prepare the meringue (see recipe, steps 1 and 2, page 338). Preheat the oven to 210°F | 100°C | gas mark ¼.

2 ••• Transfer meringue to the piping bag fitted with the ½-inch | 14-mm plain tip. On a baking sheet lined with parchment paper, pipe 8 disks of meringue in a spiral to a diameter of about 2 ⅓ inches | 6 cm. Place in oven and bake for approximately 2 hours.
Remove from oven, allow to cool and keep in an airtight container in a cool, dry place. •••

Chestnut vermicelli

3 ••· In a large bowl, thin the chestnut paste by mixing in the rum. Add the chestnut puree and chestnut cream. Stir to combine and keep in the refrigerator.

Sweetened whipped cream

4 ••· Prepare the sweetened whipped cream (see basic recipe).

Assembly

5 ••· Transfer the chestnut vermicelli mixture to the piping bag fitted with the vermicelli tip or the ⅖-inch | 10-mm plain tip (or, if you don't have either, you can use a spoon). Fill the bottom of the verrines with a ¾-inch | 2-cm thick layer of chestnut vermicelli.

Place a meringue disk on top and cover with a rosette of sweetened whipped cream.

Decorate with half of a candied chestnut.

LES GROS GÂTEAUX

Large Cakes

For 8 people

Preparation: 4 hours *Cooking time: 37 minutes* *Resting time: 2 hours and 50 minutes*

Intensément Chocolat

Intensely Chocolate

Chocolate macaron

¾ cup + 2 tbsp | 85 g ground almonds (almond flour)

⅔ cup | 80 g confectioners' (icing) sugar

1 tbsp (5 g) unsweetened cocoa powder

¾ oz | 20 g chocolate (minimum 70% cacao solids)

2 egg whites + 1 tbsp whipped egg white

⅓ cup | 70 g granulated sugar

Dark chocolate sponge cake

2 ½ tbsp (20 g) all-purpose flour

1 ½ tbsp (15 g) potato starch

2 tbsp (10 g) unsweetened cocoa powder

2 eggs

¼ cup | 50 g granulated sugar

Cocoa syrup

2 tbsp (25 g) granulated sugar

1 tbsp unsweetened cocoa powder

5 tbsp water

Dark chocolate ganache

4 ½ oz | 125 g chocolate (minimum 70% cacao solids)

½ cup | 125 ml heavy (double) cream

2 tbsp | 30 g butter

Chocolate mousse

4 eggs

3 tbsp (40 g) granulated sugar

5 ½ oz | 160 g chocolate
(minimum 70% cacao solids)

3 tbsp | 40 g butter

1 pinch of salt

Dark chocolate glaze

3 ½ oz | 100 g chocolate
(minimum 70% cacao solids)

⅓ cup | 80 ml heavy (double) cream

2 ⅔ tbsp (40 g) whole milk

1 ½ tbsp (20 g) granulated sugar

1 ½ tbsp | 20 g butter

Dark chocolate flakes for decoration

EQUIPMENT

Round ring mould 8-inch | 20-cm diameter,
1 ½ inches | 4 cm high

Piping bag fitted with a ½-inch | 10-mm plain tip

Round cardboard cake board

Pastry brush

•••

Chocolate macaron

1 ••· Prepare the batter according to the instructions for macaron shells in the chocolate macaron recipe (page 18), using the quantities of ingredients listed here. Line 2 baking sheets with parchment paper and draw an 8-inch | 20-cm diameter circle on each. Transfer macaron batter to the piping bag fitted with a plain tip and pipe a disk onto one of the sheets, filling in the drawn circle. Bake for approximately 25 minutes (at 300°F | 150°C | gas mark 2). Allow to cool.

Dark chocolate sponge cake

2 ••· Preheat the oven to 340°F | 170°C | gas mark 3.
Sift together the flour, potato starch and cocoa powder.
Separate the egg yolks and egg whites. In a bowl, lightly beat the egg yolks to liquefy.

3 ••· In a large clean, dry bowl, whip the egg whites to a foam. Once they are white and frothy, incorporate the sugar and continue to whip until firm.
Immediately add the egg yolks, lightly folding in with a rubber spatula.
Sprinkle in the flour, potato starch and cocoa powder mixture and gently combine.
Transfer batter to a clean piping bag fitted with a plain tip. On the second prepared baking sheet, pipe another 8-inch | 20-cm diameter disk. Place in oven and bake for 12 minutes.

Cocoa syrup

4 ••• In a saucepan, mix together the sugar and cocoa powder. Add the water and bring to a boil.
Allow to cool.

Dark chocolate ganache

5 ••• Using a knife, finely chop the chocolate on a cutting board and transfer to a large bowl. In a saucepan, bring the cream to a boil and pour over the chopped chocolate in 3 parts, making sure to combine well with a wooden spatula after each addition. Mix until homogenous. Cut the butter into small pieces and stir into the ganache until smooth.

Beginning of assembly

6 ••• Cut the disks of chocolate macaron and chocolate cake to fit properly in the mould.
Place a cake board the size of the mould on a round platter. Line the mould with aluminum foil to make unmoulding easier and place on the cardboard.
Place the macaron disk in the mould and pour in the ganache. Put this assembled preparation in the refrigerator.

•••

Chocolate mousse

7 ••• Follow the instructions for the chocolate mousse (page 156), using the quantities of ingredients listed here.
Remove the assembled preparation from the refrigerator. Transfer the chocolate mousse to a clean piping bag fitted with a plain tip. Pipe a thin layer of mousse in a spiral into the mould. Place the chocolate cake on top. Using a pastry brush, soak the cake with cocoa syrup.
Fill with remaining chocolate mousse to the top of the mould and smooth the surface. Refrigerate for 2 hours.
Take out of the refrigerator and remove the mould and aluminum foil. Cover cake with plastic wrap and place in the freezer for 30 minutes to chill.

Dark chocolate glaze

8 ••• Using a knife, chop the dark chocolate on a cutting board and transfer to a large bowl. In a saucepan, bring the cream, milk and sugar to a boil, then pour this hot liquid over the chopped chocolate. Add the butter and combine until smooth. Allow to cool to lukewarm.

9 ••• Place a wire rack on a clean baking sheet.
When the glaze is barely lukewarm, remove cake from the freezer and place on the rack. Remove plastic wrap. Using a ladle, immediately coat the entire cake with glaze. Use a palette knife (or offset spatula) to spread the glaze and smooth the surface. Allow to rest for 2 minutes to set.

Slide the tip of a knife between the cake board and the wire rack to slightly lift the cake. Using the knife, scrape the excess glaze off the bottom and apply chocolate flakes around the base.
Decorate the top with a line of white chocolate and dark chocolate shavings.

Chef's tip

Assemble the cake on a cake board the same size as the mould to make it easier to move from assembling platter to the rack for glazing, and to move again once the glaze is set. If you do not have a cake board, use a rigid piece of cardboard wrapped in aluminum foil.

For 8 people
Preparation: 1 ½ hours + basic recipes *Cooking time: 10 minutes* *Resting time: 2 hours*

Charlotte Framboise

Raspberry Charlotte

Ladyfingers
See recipe, page 334 and double the quantities of ingredients

Rose-flavoured syrup
See recipe in the raspberry rose verrines, page 162 and halve the quantities of ingredients

Rose Bavarian cream
See recipe in the raspberry rose verrines, page 162 and add 1 gelatin sheet
(¼ tbsp | 2 g powdered gelatin)

4 cups | 500 g raspberries
1 red rose, unsprayed

Equipment

Round ring mould, 8-inch | 20-cm diameter, 2 inches | 5 cm high
Piping bag fitted with a ⅖-inch | 10-mm plain tip
Piping bag fitted with a ½-inch | 14-mm plain tip
Pastry brush

Ladyfingers

1 ••• Line 3 baking sheets with parchment paper. On 2 of the 3 sheets, draw a 7-inch | 18-cm diameter circle. Prepare the ladyfinger batter according to the recipe (page 334), doubling the quantities of ingredients.

2 ••• Preheat the oven to 340°F | 170°C | gas mark 3.
Transfer a portion of the batter to the piping bag fitted with the ⅖-inch | 10-mm tip and pipe 35 ladyfingers 2 ⅓ x ¾-inch | 6 x 2-cm onto the baking sheet lined with a blank piece of parchment paper.
Using a fine mesh sieve or sifter, sprinkle half of the confectioners' sugar over the piped batter. Allow to rest for 10 minutes. •••

3 ••· Meanwhile, transfer remaining batter to the piping bag fitted with the ½-inch | 14-mm plain tip. Pipe 2 disks in a spiral on the prepared baking sheets, filling in the drawn circles.
Dust the tops of the 35 piped ladyfingers again with the remaining confectioners' sugar. Immediately place all 3 sheets in the oven and bake for approximately 10 minutes until lightly coloured.
Remove from oven and allow to cool.

Rose-flavoured syrup and Rose Bavarian cream

4 ••· Following the recipes in the raspberry rose verrines (page 162), prepare the syrup, halving the quantities of ingredients, as well as the Bavarian cream, adding an extra gelatin sheet for the height of the charlotte.

Assembly

5 ••· Line the mould with aluminum foil to make unmoulding easier.
If necessary, cut the baked disks of sponge cake to fit properly in the mould. They should be ⅖ inch | 1 cm thick. If they are too thick, trim as needed. Place the first disk of cake in the mould and using a pastry brush, soak very lightly with syrup. Place the ladyfingers vertically, set against the inside of the mould, the tops facing out.

6 ••• Set aside enough raspberries to cover the top of the cake.
Using a ladle, pour a thin layer of Bavarian cream into the mould and arrange several raspberries on the cream, leaving space between them. Pour in Bavarian cream again to slightly cover the raspberries. Place the second disk of cake on top and repeat the previous steps in the same order: Bavarian cream, raspberries, Bavarian cream.
Refrigerate the charlotte for 2 hours.
Decorate the surface of the cake with the remaining fresh raspberries and rose petals.

For 8 people
Preparation: 1 ½ hours + basic recipes *Cooking time: 10 minutes* *Resting time: 2 hours*

Charlotte Rhubarbe Fraises

Strawberry Rhubarb Charlotte

Rhubarb compote
8 ½ oz | 240 g rhubarb, peeled and thinly sliced
1 ½ tbsp (20 g) granulated sugar
+ 2 tbsp (25 g) granulated sugar
2 tsp (6 g) pectin (powder)
4 gelatin sheets (1 tbsp | 7 g powdered gelatin)
3 ⅓ tbsp (50 g) water

Ladyfinger sponge cake
See recipe, page 334 and double the quantities of ingredients
a few drops of green food colouring

Strawberry Bavarian cream
1 ¾ cups | 250 g strawberries
5 gelatin sheets (1 ¼ tbsp | 9 g powdered gelatin)
3 egg yolks
⅓ cup + 1 tbsp | 75 g granulated sugar
⅓ cup + 1 tbsp | 100 ml whole milk
⅔ cup | 150 ml heavy (double) cream, very cold

2 ½ cups | 375 g strawberries, medium size for assembly

EQUIPMENT
Round ring mould, 8-inch | 20-cm diameter, 2 inches | 5 cm high
Piping bag fitted with a plain ½-inch | 10-mm tip

RHUBARB COMPOTE

1 ••• Prepare the compote according to the instructions in the recipe for the rhubarb and wild strawberry tartlets (page 132), using the quantities of ingredients listed here.

LADYFINGER SPONGE CAKE

2 ••• Line 3 baking sheets with parchment paper. On 2 of the 3 sheets, draw an 8-inch | 20-cm diameter circle, and on the third sheet, draw a rectangle 12 ½ x 5-inch | 32 x 12-cm. •••

Prepare the ladyfinger batter according to the recipe (page 334), doubling the quantities of ingredients and adding a touch of green food colouring.

3 ••• Preheat the oven to 340°F | 170°C | gas mark 3.
Using an offset spatula, spread a portion of the batter inside the drawn rectangle to a thickness of ⅕ inch | 5 mm. Transfer the remaining batter to the piping bag fitted with a plain tip, and pipe 2 disks in a spiral on the prepared baking sheets, filling in the drawn circles. Immediately place all 3 sheets in the oven and bake for approximately 10 minutes. Remove from oven and allow to cool.

Strawberry Bavarian cream

4 ••• Place a large mixing bowl in the freezer to chill.
Wash the strawberries, drain on a dish towel and hull.
Put the gelatin sheets in a small bowl of very cold water. Allow to soften for 10 minutes.
In a large bowl, whisk the egg yolks and sugar until slightly pale.
Drain the gelatin sheets, squeezing out all excess liquid, and set aside.

5 ••• In a saucepan, bring the milk to a simmer. Pour a third of the hot milk over the egg yolk and sugar mixture (to temper the yolks). Whisk together and pour the whole mixture back into the saucepan. Cook over low heat, stirring constantly with a wooden spoon until the custard thickens. It should coat the spoon when ready; if you run your finger down the back

of the spoon, the custard should not run back into the line. Important: the custard should never come to a boil. (It should cook at a maximum of 185°F | 85°C.)
As soon as the custard has this consistency, remove from heat and add the drained gelatin to stop the cooking. Pour into a large bowl. Continue to stir for 5 minutes so that the Bavarian cream stays smooth. Allow to cool completely.
Add the hulled strawberries, and using an immersion hand blender or electric mixer, blend together. Keep in the refrigerator just long enough for the Bavarian cream to begin to set.

Beginning of assembly

6 ••• Line the mould with aluminum foil to make unmoulding easier.
Turn out the rectangular cake onto a sheet of parchment paper and carefully peel off the parchment paper used during baking. Slice two strips, 2 inches | 5 cm wide. Place the first strip around the inside of the mould, keeping it straight, following the edge, then place the second strip to continue around the inside of the mould. Trim the excess with a small knife.

7 ••• If necessary, cut the baked disks of sponge cake to fit properly in the mould. They should be ⅖ inch | 1 cm thick. If they are too thick, trim as needed. Place the first disk of cake in the mould. Fill with the jellied rhubarb compote and keep in the refrigerator.

•••

Final steps for Bavarian cream and assembly

8 ••• Remove the chilled bowl from the freezer. Pour in the very cold heavy cream and whisk energetically until it thickens and becomes firm.
Mix the strawberry Bavarian cream, barely set, until smooth. Using a rubber spatula, gently fold in the whipped cream.
Keep at room temperature.

9 ••• Wash the strawberries (for assembly), drain on a dish towel and hull.
Slice ⅞ cup | 125 g of the strawberries to a thickness of ⅕ inch | 5 mm.
Remove the assembled preparation from the refrigerator. Using a ladle, pour a thin layer of Bavarian cream halfway up the mould and place the second disk of sponge cake (⅖ inch | 1 cm thick) on top. Arrange the strawberry slices on the cake and lightly cover with Bavarian cream, keeping below the edge of the mould.
Refrigerate for 2 hours.
Slice the remaining 1 ¾ cup | 250 g of strawberries in half and arrange in a decorative pattern on top of the cake.

L

For 8 people   Preparation: 1 ½ hours + basic recipe
Cooking time: 1 hour and 50 minutes   Resting time: 2 ½ hours

Duchesse

Duchesse

Meringue ladyfingers
See recipe, page 338 prepared with:
½ cup | 60 g confectioners' (icing) sugar
2 egg whites
⅓ cup | 60 g granulated sugar

Soft walnut cake
1 cup | 80 g walnut halves
½ cup + 1 tbsp | 65 g confectioners' (icing) sugar
3 ½ tbsp (30 g) cake flour
⅓ cup + 1 tbsp | 35 g ground almonds (almond flour)
4 egg whites
¼ cup packed | 50 g light brown sugar

Chestnut cream
2 oz | 50 g chestnut paste
1 tsp rum
3 ½ oz | 100 g unsweetened chestnut puree
2 oz | 50 g chestnut cream

Chestnut mousse
1 ½ cups | 360 ml heavy (double) cream, very cold
2 gelatin sheets (½ tbsp | 4 g powdered gelatin)
3 ½ oz | 100 g chestnut paste
2 tbsp walnut liqueur
1 oz | 30 g chestnut puree
1 oz | 30 g chestnut cream

5 ½ oz | 150 g crumbled candied chestnuts for assembly

Milk chocolate glaze
5 ½ oz | 150 g milk chocolate (39% cacao solids)
¼ cup | 60 ml heavy (double) cream
2 tbsp (30 g) whole milk
1 ¼ tbsp (15 g) granulated sugar
1 tbsp | 15 g butter

1 whole candied chestnut for decoration

Equipment
Piping bag fitted with a ⅓-inch | 8-mm plain tip
Piping bag fitted with a ½-inch | 10-mm plain tip
Round ring mould, 8-inch | 20-cm diameter,
1 ½ inches | 4 cm high
Round cardboard cake board

•••

Meringue ladyfingers

1 ••· Preheat the oven to 210°F | 100°C | gas mark ¼.
Prepare meringue (page 338) and transfer to the piping bag fitted with the ⅓-inch | 8-mm plain tip. Pipe strips 1 ½ x ⅖-inch | 4 x 1-cm onto a baking sheet lined with parchment paper. Pipe a total of 65 meringues to cover the 25-inch | 63-cm exterior of the cake. To make this easier, draw 3 rows of 2 parallel lines on the parchment paper. Leave space between the rows, and 1 ½ inches | 4 cm between each of the 2 parallel lines. You can then pipe 1 ½-inch | 4-cm perpendicular strips of meringue. Using a fine mesh sieve or sifter, sprinkle with half of the confectioners' sugar.

2 ••· Allow to rest 5 minutes and dust again with the remaining confectioners' sugar. Immediately place sheet in oven and bake for approximately 1 ½ hours. The meringues should bake slowly and gradually dry out. Watch that they do not darken too quickly.
Allow to cool completely and keep in an airtight container.

Soft walnut cake

3 ••· Line 2 baking sheets with parchment paper. Draw an 8-inch | 20-cm diameter circle on each.
On a cutting board, roughly chop the walnut halves into pieces smaller than ⅕ inch | 5 mm, in order to pass through the ½-inch | 10-mm tip on the piping bag.
Sift the confectioners' sugar and flour into a large bowl. Add the ground almonds and chopped walnuts, and toss together.

4 ••• In a clean, dry bowl, whip the egg whites to a foam. Once they are frothy, add the brown sugar and continue to whip until sugar is dissolved. Using a rubber spatula, gently fold the dry mixture into the whipped egg whites.
Preheat the oven to 340°F | 170°C | gas mark 3.
Transfer the batter to the piping bag fitted with the ½-inch | 10-mm plain tip. Pipe 2 disks in a spiral on the prepared baking sheets, filling in the drawn circles. Place in oven and bake for 20 minutes.
Remove from oven and allow to cool.

Chestnut cream

5 ••• Thin the chestnut cream by mixing in the rum. Add the chestnut puree and the chestnut cream.

Chestnut mousse

6 ••• Place a large mixing bowl in the freezer to chill. Keep the heavy cream in the refrigerator until ready to use.
Put the gelatin sheets in a small bowl of very cold water. Allow to soften for 10 minutes.
Thin the chestnut paste by mixing in the walnut liqueur. Add the chestnut puree and the chestnut cream.

•••

7 ••· Drain the gelatin sheets, squeezing hard to remove all excess liquid. In a small saucepan, bring 2 ½ tbsp (40 ml) of heavy cream to a simmer. Add the softened gelatin. Put ¼ of the chestnut mixture in a bowl. If it is cold, bring to room temperature in the microwave or over a pan of gently simmering water. Add the hot cream, then pour the entire mixture back over the remaining chestnut mixture.

8 ••· Put the remaining heavy cream (1 ⅓ cups | 320 ml) in the chilled bowl, and using an electric mixer if possible, whip energetically until firm. Using a rubber spatula, gently fold the whipped cream into the chestnut mixture, in 3 parts.

Assembly

9 ••· Place a cake board the size of the mould on a round platter. Line the mould with aluminum foil to make unmoulding easier and place on the cardboard.

Cut the disks of walnut cake to fit properly in the mould. Place a first disk in the mould. Transfer the chestnut mousse to the piping bag fitted with the ½-inch | 10-mm plain tip. Fill the mould halfway up with mousse. Sprinkle the crumbled chestnut pieces over the entire surface.

10••• Using a spoon, spread the chestnut cream over the second disk of walnut cake in an even layer. Place in the mould and fill with the remaining chestnut mousse to the very top. Smooth the surface.
Refrigerate for 2 hours, then carefully remove the mould. Cover the cake in plastic wrap and freeze for 30 minutes to chill.

Milk chocolate glaze

11 ••• Using a knife, chop the chocolate on a cutting board and transfer to a large bowl. In a saucepan, bring the cream, milk and sugar to a boil, then pour this hot liquid over the chopped chocolate. Add the butter and mix together until smooth. Allow to cool to lukewarm.
Place a wire rack on a clean baking sheet.
When the glaze is barely lukewarm, remove cake from the freezer and place on the rack. Remove plastic wrap and using a ladle, immediately coat the entire cake with glaze. Use a palette knife (or offset spatula) to spread the glaze and smooth the surface.
Allow to rest for 2 minutes to set, then place on a serving platter. Decorate the exterior of the cake with the meringues (as seen in the photo) and top with a candied chestnut.

Chef's tip

Assemble the cake on a cake board the same size as the mould to make it easier to move from assembling platter to the rack for glazing, and to move again after the glaze is set. If you do not have a cake board, use a rigid piece of cardboard wrapped in aluminum foil.

For 8 people

Preparation: 2 hours *Cooking time: 25 minutes* *Resting time: 1 hour*

Divin

Divin

Almond sponge cake with nougat

1 cup | 100 g ground almonds (almond flour)

⅔ cup | 80 g confectioners' (icing) sugar

⅓ cup | 40 g cake flour

5 egg whites

½ cup + 1 tbsp | 110 g granulated sugar

1 oz | 25 g nougat pieces

Nougat mousseline cream

9 tbsp | 125 g butter

1 cup + 1 tbsp | 250 ml whole milk

2 egg yolks

⅓ cup + 1 tbsp | 75 g granulated sugar

3 tbsp (25 g) cornstarch (cornflour)

7 oz | 200 g nougat cream

4 oz | 110 g nougat pieces

Jellied raspberry coulis

2 gelatin sheets (½ tbsp | 4 g powdered gelatin)

½ lemon

2 ¼ cups | 300 g raspberries

2 ⅔ tbsp (35 g) granulated sugar

3 tbsp water

3 cups | 375 g raspberries

Confectioners' (icing) sugar for dusting

Equipment

Piping bag fitted with a ½-inch | 10-mm plain tip

Almond sponge cake with nougat

1 ••• Line 2 baking sheets with parchment paper and draw a 9-inch | 22 ½-cm diameter circle on each.

2 ••• In a large bowl, mix together the ground almonds, confectioners' sugar and flour.

•••

In another clean, dry bowl, whip the egg whites to a foam. Once they are frothy, add the granulated sugar and continue to whip until sugar is dissolved. Using a rubber spatula, gently fold the dry mixture into the whipped egg whites.

3 ••· Preheat the oven to 340°F | 170°C | gas mark 3.
Transfer batter to the piping bag fitted with a plain tip. On each prepared baking sheet, pipe a disk of batter in a spiral, filling in the drawn circles. Sprinkle with pieces of nougat.
Place sheets in oven and bake for 20 minutes. Remove from oven and allow to cool.

Nougat mousseline cream

4 ••· Remove the butter from the refrigerator to soften.
In a saucepan, bring the milk to a simmer.
In a large bowl, whisk the egg yolks and sugar until slightly pale. Incorporate the cornstarch. Pour a third of the hot milk over the mixture of egg yolks, sugar and cornstarch (to temper the yolks). Whisk together and pour the whole mixture back into the saucepan. Bring to a boil while stirring with a whisk, making sure to scrape down the sides of the pan with a spatula.

5 ••· Remove from heat and allow to cool for 10 minutes so that it is hot but not boiling. Incorporate half of the butter. Pour cream into a baking dish, cover with plastic wrap and allow to cool.

Jellied raspberry coulis

6 ••• Place the gelatin sheets in a small bowl of very cold water. Allow to soften for 10 minutes.

Juice the lemon half and set aside.

Using an immersion hand blender or food processor, blend the raspberries with the sugar until you have a liquid consistency. Strain the mixture through a fine mesh sieve; alternate pressing and scraping with a spoon to obtain as much pulp as possible without the raspberry seeds. To make this easier, just before all of the raspberry puree has been strained, add the lemon juice and water to the sieve, which will pass through with any remaining raspberry pulp.

7 ••• In a saucepan, heat ¼ of this preparation to lukewarm. Drain the gelatin sheets, squeezing hard to remove all excess liquid. Add gelatin to the saucepan and stir to melt. Pour this mixture over the remaining ¾ of cold raspberry pulp. Stir to combine and refrigerate for 30 minutes for the coulis to set.

Final steps for nougat mousseline cream

8 ••• The mousseline cream should be at room temperature. If it is still hot, refrigerate for 10 minutes to finish cooling off.

In a large bowl, whip the mousseline cream with an electric mixer until smooth. Add the nougat cream and the remaining half of the butter. Whip until emulsified and smooth. Add the pieces of nougat.

•••

ASSEMBLY

9 ••• Set aside raspberries to decorate the top of the cake.
Place the first disk of almond cake on a platter. Transfer the mousseline cream to the piping bag fitted with a plain tip. Pipe a thin layer of cream on the cake in a spiral. Place raspberries on the cream, starting at the edge and working in towards the center. Lightly press down, to push up the cream between the raspberries.

10 ••• Using a palette knife (or offset spatula), cover the raspberries with mousseline cream to create a flat surface. Pipe a neat ring of cream around the border. Freeze for 10 minutes. Pour in a layer of jellied coulis to a thickness of about ¼ inch | 5-6 mm. Refrigerate to set.
Turn the second disk of almond cake upside down. Coat with a thin layer of mousseline cream and turn over into the mould, for the cream to rest on the jellied coulis.
Dust lightly with confectioners' sugar and decorate with raspberries.
Keep in the refrigerator.

Chef's tip

Remove the cake from the refrigerator 20 minutes before serving.
Serve with raspberry coulis.

For 8 people

Preparation: 2 hours + basic recipe *Cooking time: 30 minutes* *Resting time: 2 hours*

Fraisier, Framboisier

Fraisier (and Framboisier)

Almond génoise cake

3 ½ tbsp | 50 g butter

+ 1 ½ tbsp butter for cake pan

1 ⅔ cups | 200 g cake flour

+ 2 ½ tbsp cake flour for cake pan

6 eggs

1 cup | 200 g granulated sugar

½ cup | 50 g ground almonds (almond flour)

Kirsch syrup

½ cup - 1 tbsp | 100 ml water

½ cup | 100 g granulated sugar

2 ½ tbsp (40 ml) kirsch liqueur

2 ½ tbsp (40 ml) raspberry liqueur

Pistachio mousseline cream

See basic recipe

4 ⅔ cups | 700 g strawberries

Pistachio almond paste

1 cup | 250 g almond paste

1 ½ tbsp (25 g) pistachio paste

EQUIPMENT

Round cake pan with straight sides, 8 ½ to 9-inch | 21 to 22-cm diameter

Round ring mould, 8-inch | 20-cm diameter

Piping bag fitted with a ½-inch | 10-mm plain tip

Pastry brush

Rolling pin

ALMOND GÉNOISE AND KIRSCH SYRUP

1 ••• Melt the 1 ½ tbsp of butter. Using a pastry brush, butter the cake pan. Refrigerate for 15 minutes for the butter to harden. Sift the flour. In a small saucepan, melt the 3 ½ tbsp | 50 g of butter over low heat. •••

2 ••· In a large heatproof mixing bowl, whisk together the eggs and sugar. Preheat the oven to 340°F | 170°C | gas mark 3.
Place the mixing bowl over a pan of gently simmering water and whisk until the mixture is warm (approximately 122°F | 50°C), thick and pale, and has tripled in volume. This should take 10 minutes with an electric mixer and 15 minutes with a whisk. Remove from heat and continue to beat until the mixture has completely cooled down.

3 ••· Using a rubber spatula, fold in the sifted flour little by little, then the ground almonds and the melted butter. To gently mix together, start with the spatula in the center of the bowl, work up the sides of the bowl and bring back down towards the center, all the while turning the bowl regularly. This will result in a smooth and homogenous mixture.
Lightly flour the cake pan and turn upside down to tap out any excess. Immediately fill with batter, place in oven and bake for approximately 30 minutes.

4 ••· While the génoise is baking, prepare the kirsch syrup.
In a saucepan, bring the water and sugar to a boil. Allow to cool.
Pour the kirsch and raspberry liqueur into the cooled syrup.
Check to see if the génoise is done by inserting the tip of a knife into the center. When the cake is ready, the knife should come out clean, dry and free of crumbs.
Remove from oven, allow to cool for 5 minutes before removing from the mould and placing on a rack. Allow to cool completely.

Pistachio mousseline cream

5 ••• Prepare the mousseline cream (see basic recipe), steps 1 to 3 and allow to cool.
Meanwhile, wash the strawberries, drain on a dish towel and hull.
In a large bowl, whip the cooled mousseline cream with an electric mixer until smooth. Add the pistachio paste and the remaining half of the butter. Whip until emulsified and smooth.

Assembly

6 ••• Using a serrated knife, remove the darkened layer of génoise, then slice horizontally to create two disks of cake, ⅖ inch | 1 cm thick. Cut the disks to fit properly in the mould (you can place the mould on top of the cake and push down).

7 ••• Place the mould on a platter and add the first disk of génoise. Lightly soak with kirsch syrup. Transfer the mousseline cream to the piping bag fitted with a plain tip. Pipe a layer of cream in a spiral on top of the cake. Arrange a border of strawberries (sliced in half) around the inside of the mould, cut side out (against the mould), for a final presentation as seen in the photo.
Fill the center with whole strawberries, pushing down on the cream so that it rises between the strawberries. Cover with mousseline cream, filling the gaps and creating a flat surface. Place the second disk of génoise on the cream. Lightly soak with syrup. Fill with the remaining mousseline cream to the very edge of the mould and smooth the surface. •••

Pistachio almond paste for top of cake

8 ••• Using your hands, mix the almond paste with the pistachio paste. On a clean work surface, using a rolling pin, roll out this mixture extremely thin (1 mm). Cover the cake with this sheet and trim the excess. Refrigerate cake for 2 hours.
Carefully remove the mould and decorate the cake with the remaining strawberries, sliced in half.

Variation

To prepare a Framboisier, replace the 4 ⅔ cups | 700 g of strawberries with 5 ⅔ cups | 700 g of raspberries.

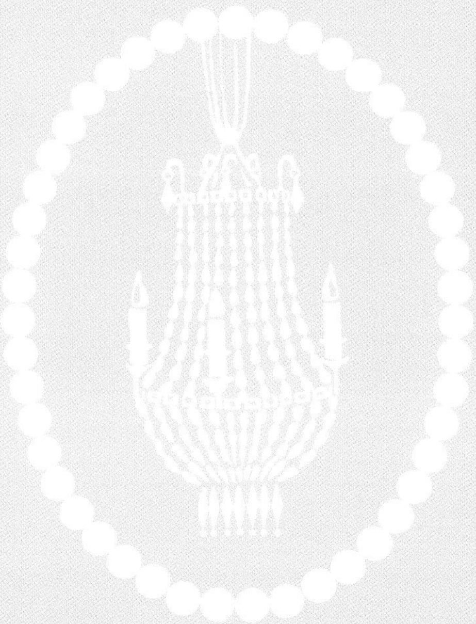

For 8 people

Preparation: 2 hours + basic recipe   *Cooking time: 20 to 25 minutes*

Harmonie

Harmonie

Pistachio macaron

1 ½ cups | 150 g ground almonds (almond flour)

⅔ cup | 75 g shelled raw pistachios

1 ¾ cups | 210 g confectioners' (icing) sugar

5 egg whites + 1 egg white

¾ cup + 2 tbsp | 175 g granulated sugar

a few drops of green food colouring

Pistachio mousseline cream

See basic recipe

⅓ cup | 40 g shelled raw pistachios

2 ¾ cups | 400 g strawberries

¾ cup | 100 g raspberries

Equipment

Piping bag fitted with a ½-inch | 10-mm plain tip

Pistachio macaron

1 ••• Line 2 baking sheets with parchment paper and draw a 10-inch | 25-cm diameter circle on each.

Combine the ground almonds, pistachios and confectioners' sugar in a food processor and pulse to obtain a fine powder. Sift or strain through a sieve to remove any lumps.

2 ••• In a clean, dry bowl, whisk the 5 egg whites to a foam. Once they are frothy, add a third of the granulated sugar and whip until sugar is dissolved; add another third of the granulated sugar, whip for another minute; finally add the remaining granulated sugar and whip for 1 more minute. Using a rubber spatula, delicately fold the sifted mixture of •••

ground almonds, pistachios and confectioners' sugar into the whipped egg whites. In a separate small bowl, beat the remaining 1 egg white until just frothy. Then add to the final mixture, along with a few drops of green food colouring, folding gently to slightly loosen the batter.

3 ••· Transfer the mixture to the piping bag fitted with a plain tip. On one of the baking sheets, pipe a neat ring of macaron batter, following the drawn circle, which will serve as the border of the cake. On the other prepared baking sheet, pipe a disk of batter in a spiral, filling in the drawn circle.

Preheat the oven to 325°F | 160°C | gas mark 3.

Allow the piped batter to rest uncovered for 10 minutes before placing in the oven so it forms a slight crust. Place sheets in oven and bake the macaron ring for approximately 15 minutes and the disk for 20 to 25 minutes.

Remove from oven and allow to cool. Do not try to remove the macaron ring from the baking sheet when still warm; it will break.

Pistachio mousseline cream

4 ••· Prepare the mousseline cream (see basic recipe), steps 1 to 3 and allow to cool. Meanwhile, on a cutting board or in a small food processor, chop the pistachios.

Wash the strawberries, drain on a dish towel and hull.

5 ••• In a large bowl, whip the cooled mousseline cream with an electric mixer until smooth. Add the pistachio paste and the remaining half of the butter. Whip until emulsified and smooth. Fold in the chopped pistachios.

Assembly

6 ••• Place the macaron disk upside down on a serving platter. Transfer mousseline cream to the piping bag fitted with a plain tip, and pipe a ⅕-inch | ½-cm thick layer in a spiral.
Carefully remove the macaron ring from the baking sheet and place gently on the cream.
Slice the strawberries in half lengthwise and arrange in a decorative pattern in the center. Top with raspberries.

Chef's tip
Serve with strawberry or raspberry coulis and pistachio ice cream.

For 8 people

Preparation: 1 ½ hours + basic recipes *Resting time: 2 hours*

Millefeuille Praliné

Praline Millefeuille (Napoleon)

Caramelized puff pastry

See basic recipe

Praline mousseline cream

See basic recipe

Caramelized almonds and hazelnuts

2 tbsp water

⅓ cup | 70 g granulated sugar

⅓ cup | 50 g whole almonds

⅓ cup | 50 g whole hazelnuts

Crisp caramelized almond and hazelnut praline

1 oz | 35 g milk chocolate

¾ tbsp | 10 g butter

5 ½ oz | 150 g almond and hazelnut praline

2 oz | 60 g crêpes dentelles
(or other thin crisp butter wafers)

Brown sugar for decoration

Equipment

Candy thermometer

Piping bag fitted with a ½-inch | 10-mm plain tip

Caramelized puff pastry

1 ••• Prepare the caramelized puff pastry (see basic recipe) in advance to obtain 3 rectangles 7 x 9 ½-inch | 18 x 24-cm.

Praline mousseline cream

2 ••• Prepare the mousseline cream (see basic recipe), steps 1 to 3, and allow to cool.

•••

Caramelized almonds and hazelnuts

3 ••• In a saucepan, bring the water and sugar to a boil and cook for 2 minutes (to 244°F | 118°C if you have a candy thermometer). Add the almonds and hazelnuts and stir together off heat until the sugar starts to resemble coarse sand. Return to medium heat and gently stir just until the sugar coating the nuts has caramelized.

Remove from heat and using a spatula, spread the almonds and hazelnuts on a piece of parchment paper. Be very careful as the caramel is extremely hot. Allow to cool.

Crisp caramelized almond and hazelnut praline

4 ••• Using a knife, chop the chocolate on a cutting board. Cut the butter into pieces.

Put chocolate and butter in a heatproof bowl set over a pan of gently simmering water or in the microwave at medium power, and melt very gently. Remove from heat; the mixture must be lukewarm for the following steps.

Add the praline, then crumble the crêpes dentelles and add to the mixture. Pour onto a sheet of parchment paper and spread out to a 7 x 9 ½-inch | 18 x 24-cm rectangle (create straight lines for presentation). Freeze to make pulling off paper easier.

Final steps for praline mousseline cream and assembly

5 ••• In a large bowl, whip the cooled mousseline cream with an electric mixer until smooth. Add the praline pastes and the remaining half of the butter. Whip again until emulsified and smooth.

6 ••· Cut out 3 rectangles of caramelized puff pastry 7 x 9 ½-inch | 18 x 24-cm. It is essential that you have 2 whole pieces that are perfectly rectangular and cut straight. One will be the top of the millefeuille, the other will be the bottom that you place on the serving platter. The third piece in the middle can be made of several broken pieces fit together.
Using a knife, roughly crush the caramelized almonds and hazelnuts.

7 ••· Transfer the praline mousseline cream to the piping bag fitted with a plain tip. Pipe 9 oz | 250 g of cream over the bottom layer of puff pastry. Sprinkle with crushed caramelized almonds and hazelnuts.
Place the second rectangle of puff pastry and top with 4 ½ oz | 125 g of cream. Place the layer of crisp praline on the cream, turning it upside down, so you can simply peel off the parchment paper once it is in place. Pipe another 4 ½ oz | 125 g of the remaining mousseline cream on the praline and top with the last rectangle of puff pastry.
Decorate with brown sugar. Keep in the refrigerator until ready to serve.

Les Viennoiseries

Pastries

Makes 12 individual brioches (2 oz | 60 g) or 24 mini brioches (1 oz | 30 g)
Preparation: 30 minutes + basic recipe   Cooking time: 15 minutes   Resting time: 2 ½ hours

Brioches au Sucre

Brioches

26 ½ oz | 750 g brioche dough: see basic recipe
2 ½ tbsp all-purpose flour for work surface
1 egg
3 oz | 80 g pearl sugar

1 ••• On a floured work surface, roll out the dough in the shape of a log. Divide into pieces of equal size, weighing approximately 2 oz | 50 g.

2 ••• Using the palm of your hand, flatten each piece and fold it back over itself to form a tight ball.
Place the rounds of dough on a baking sheet lined with parchment paper and allow to rest at room temperature.
Allow the dough to double in volume (approximately 2 ½ hours). The higher the temperature (without exceeding 86°F | 30°C), the faster it will rise.

3 ••• Preheat the oven to 350°F | 180°C | gas mark 4.
Beat the egg in a small bowl and using a pastry brush, brush the dough.
Decorate the tops with pearl sugar.
Place sheet in oven and bake for 12 to 15 minutes until golden.

4 ••• Remove from oven. Allow to cool slightly and serve warm.

Chef's tip
When the dough is left to rise, cover with a damp dish towel to prevent it from forming a crust.

Makes 8 bostocks *Preparation: 1 hour + basic recipe* *Cooking time: 12 minutes*

Bostocks

Bostocks

Orange flower-scented syrup

1 cup | 250 ml water

1 ¾ cups + 2 tbsp | 375 g granulated sugar

⅓ cup | 30 g ground almonds (almond flour)

1 ⅔ tbsp (25 g) orange flower water

Brioche

1 round (mousseline) brioche, 8 inches | 20 cm high or 1 rectangular (Nanterre) brioche, 8 inches | 20 cm long

5 tbsp dark aged rum (rhum agricole if possible)

Almond cream

5 ½ oz | 160 g almond cream: see basic recipe

1 cup | 100 g sliced (flaked) almonds

Confectioners' (icing) sugar for dusting

EQUIPMENT

Piping bag fitted with a ½-inch | 10-mm plain tip

ORANGE FLOWER-SCENTED SYRUP

1 ••• In a saucepan, bring the water, sugar and ground almonds to a boil. Remove from heat and add the orange flower water.

BRIOCHE

2 ••• Cut ¾-inch | 2-cm thick slices of brioche.

Place a rack on a rimmed baking sheet. Using a skimmer (or slotted spoon), quickly dip the brioche slices one by one into the warm syrup to soak. Drain on the rack and allow to cool.

Transfer the brioche slices to another baking sheet lined with parchment paper or aluminum foil. Lightly splash with rum. •••

Almond cream

3 ••· Prepare the almond cream (see basic recipe). Preheat the oven to 340°F | 170°C | gas mark 3. Spoon the almond cream into the piping bag with a plain tip. Cover brioche slices with a thin layer of cream, 1⁄10 inch | 2 mm thick. Sprinkle with sliced almonds.

4 ••· Place sheet in oven and bake for approximately 12 minutes. Allow to cool completely, then dust with confectioners' sugar. Serve bostocks the same day they are prepared.

Makes 12 small kouglofs or 2 large kouglofs
Preparation: 1 ½ hours + basic recipe *Cooking time: 20 to 40 minutes* *Resting time: 7 ½ hours*

Kouglof

Kouglof

Brioche
1 cup | 150 g golden seedless raisins (sultanas)
26 ½ oz | 750 g brioche dough: see basic recipe
3 ½ tbsp | 50 g butter for moulds
+ 3 ½ tbsp | 50 g butter for kouglofs

Orange flower-scented syrup
8 cups | 2 litres water
1 ½ cups | 300 g granulated sugar
¼ cup | 25 g ground almonds (almond flour)
1 ⅓ tbsp (20 g) orange flower water

Sliced (flaked) almonds for large moulds
Confectioners' (icing) sugar for dusting

EQUIPMENT
12 individual kouglof moulds or 2 large kouglof moulds with a 7 ½-inch | 19-cm diameter
(Bundt pans can also be used)
Pastry brush

BRIOCHE

1 ••• Place raisins in a bowl of hot water and allow to soak for 1 hour. Meanwhile, prepare the brioche dough, following steps 1 and 2 in the basic recipe. Knead the dough until ready, then add the raisins (drained and dried on a dish towel).

2 ••• As you do for brioche dough, transfer the kouglof dough to a large bowl and cover with a damp dish towel or plastic wrap, and keep at room temperature. Allow the dough to double in volume (approx. 2 ½ hours). Return the dough to its initial volume by folding it back on itself. Refrigerate for 2 ½ hours; while chilling, it will once again rise. Deflate it again by folding it back on itself. The dough is then ready to use. •••

3 ••· Butter the moulds. If making large kouglofs, sprinkle the inside of the large moulds with sliced almonds.
Weigh out 2 ½ oz | 70 g portions for individual kouglofs, or simply divide the dough in half for larger kouglofs. Press down on each piece of dough to slightly flatten it and bring the edges toward the center to form a ball. Dip your thumb in flour and press down in the center of each ball, turn upside down and place in moulds.
Allow the dough to double in volume again (approx. 2 ½ hours) at room temperature. The higher the temperature (without exceeding 86°F | 30°C), the faster it will rise.

Orange flower-scented syrup

4 ••· In a saucepan, bring the water and sugar to a boil. Remove from heat and immediately add the ground almonds. Stir to combine. Allow to cool to lukewarm and incorporate the orange flower water.

Kouglofs

5 ••· Preheat the oven to 350°F | 180°C | gas mark 4. Place moulds in oven and bake individual kouglofs for 20 minutes or large kouglofs for 40 minutes. Remove from oven and allow to cool for 5 minutes.
Remove kouglofs from moulds and place lukewarm syrup in a bowl. Roll the pastries around in the warm syrup, or place on a wire rack and drizzle syrup over them several times.
Melt the remaining butter. Using a pastry brush, brush kouglofs so that they stay soft and moist. Dust with confectioners' sugar and serve.

L

Makes 12 individual kouign amann

Preparation: 1 hour *Cooking time: 25 minutes* *Resting time: 3 hours and 15 minutes*

Kouign Amann

Kouign Amann

2 cups | 250 g cake flour
3 ⅓ tbsp (25 g) buckwheat flour
1 tsp fleur de sel (or other coarse sea salt)
⅙ oz | 5 g fresh yeast
¾ cup | 175 ml water
1 cup | 225 g butter, very cold
+ 1 ½ tbsp butter for moulds
1 cup + 2 tbsp | 225 g granulated sugar

Equipment

Round ring moulds, 3 ½-inch | 9-cm diameter
Rolling pin

1 ••• Pour both flours into a large bowl. Place the salt on one side of the flour and the fresh yeast broken up in little pieces (using your fingers) on the other side. Important: the yeast must not come in contact with the salt before you start to mix the dough; otherwise it will lose its properties. Add the water and mix just until homogenous. Allow the dough to rise for 1 hour at room temperature.

2 ••• Place the chilled butter on a piece of parchment paper, and using a rolling pin, pound on it to soften. Using the parchment paper to help you, fold the butter back on itself and continue to soften. It must have the same consistency as the dough.

•••

3 ••• Roll out the dough to a rectangle approximately 8 x 23 ½-inch | 20 x 60-cm. Cover ⅔ of the length of the rolled dough with the butter. Fold the third of the dough without butter in towards the center, placing it on the butter. Then fold in the other (buttered) third on top of that (like a business letter). Allow to rest in the refrigerator for 30 minutes.
Roll out this package of butter and dough (the pâton) into a rectangle. Fold in thirds and allow to rest in the refrigerator again for 30 minutes.

4 ••• On a work surface sprinkled with granulated sugar, roll out the dough and sprinkle the dough itself with sugar. Fold in thirds. Allow to rest in the refrigerator for 30 minutes.
Making sure there is always sugar on the top and bottom of the dough, roll out a final time to a thickness of ⅙ inch | 4 mm, to finish with a thin sheet of pastry approximately 9 x 21 ½-inch | 22 x 55-cm. Cut out squares of dough 4 ½ x 4 ½-inch | 11 x 11-cm.

Chef's tip
Kouign amann are best served the day they are prepared to optimize taste and texture. Serve at room temperature.

5 ••• Butter the moulds. For each kouign amann, fold the 4 corners of the square of dough into the center, and press down lightly with the palm of your hand. Gently refold the newly formed corners slightly in towards the center, and once again press down lightly with your palm.
Preheat the oven to 350°F | 180°C | gas mark 4.
Place each piece of dough in the buttered moulds, and allow to double in volume for about 45 minutes.
Place in oven and bake for approximately 25 minutes.

Makes 20 doughnuts
Preparation: 1 hour *Cooking time: 3 to 4 minutes* *Resting time: 4 ½ hours*

Beignets Framboise

Raspberry Jam Doughnuts

Raspberry jam
1 cup | 250 g raspberry jam: see recipe for raspberry macarons, page 24

Leavener
2 cups + 2 tbsp | 265 g cake flour
⅙ oz | 5 g fresh yeast
¾ cup - 1 tsp | 170 ml water

Doughnut batter
1 ¾ cups + 1 tbsp | 235 g cake flour
+ 2 ½ tbsp cake flour
⅓ cup | 65 g granulated sugar
2 oz | 60 g fresh yeast
2 tsp (10 g) salt
5 egg yolks
3 ⅓ tbsp (50 ml) whole milk
4 ½ tbsp | 65 g butter, softened

Sugar decoration
¼ cup | 50 g granulated sugar
⅛ tsp (2 pinches) ground cinnamon

EQUIPMENT
Piping bag fitted with a ½-inch | 10-mm plain tip
Fryer (or heavy pan and thermometer)

Prepare the raspberry jam in advance.

LEAVENER

1 ••• Place the flour in a large bowl. Dilute the yeast in the water (lukewarm), and pour over the flour. Mix together.
Allow to double in volume at room temperature for approximately 1 hour.

•••

Doughnut batter

2 ••· Place the flour and sugar in a large bowl. Add the yeast and salt on separate sides of the flour, making sure they do not come in contact before you are ready to mix. Add the egg yolks and milk. Immediately mix together just to combine, until the batter pulls away from the sides of the bowl. Add the softened butter. Incorporate the prepared leavener (step 1) and combine until completely homogenous.
Allow the batter to double in volume for 1 hour. Slap the dough down in the bowl to deflate and form a ball. Refrigerate for 30 minutes.

Doughnuts

3 ••· Once the dough is chilled, weigh out 2 oz | 50 g portions. Fold the dough back on itself to form rounds. Place on a floured dish towel and leave in a warm spot (77°F to 86°F | 25°C to 30°C) so that they will double in volume. Allow to rest for approximately 1 ½ hours.

4 ••· Preheat the fryer to 325°F to 340°F | 160°C to 170°C. Carefully lower the doughnut rounds into the hot oil.
Cook both sides until golden brown (3 to 4 minutes). Use a skimmer (or slotted spoon) to remove doughnuts from oil and drain on paper towel.

5 ••· Allow to cool completely. Spoon the raspberry jam into the piping bag fitted with a plain tip, and pipe jam into each doughnut.
Toss the sugar and cinnamon together, and roll the doughnuts in the mixture to coat.

Makes 20 bugnes
Preparation: 30 minutes *Cooking time: 2 to 3 minutes* *Resting time: 1 hour*

Bugnes

Bugnes

1 lemon, unwaxed
2 tbsp (25 g) granulated sugar
⅛ tsp (2 pinches) fleur de sel (or other coarse sea salt)
1 tbsp orange flower water
2 eggs
5 tbsp | 75 g butter
2 cups | 250 g cake flour
+ 2 ½ tbsp cake flour for work surface
Confectioners' (icing) sugar for dusting

EQUIPMENT

Grater
Rolling pin
Fryer (or heavy pan and thermometer)
Fluted wheel (optional)

1 ••• Using a grater, remove the zest from the lemon and toss with the sugar in a small bowl.
In another bowl, dissolve the salt in the orange flower water, and set aside.
Remove the eggs from the refrigerator and bring to room temperature.

2 ••• Place the butter in a large heatproof bowl set over a pan of gently simmering water or in the microwave. Soften until creamy, without allowing it to melt.
Add the sugar and zest mixture and whisk until creamy. Incorporate the eggs one at a time, then add the salt and orange flower water mixture.
Add the flour and combine just until homogenous.
Allow the dough to rest for 1 hour.

•••

3 ••· Divide the dough into 2 or 3 pieces (smaller portions will be easier to roll out). Using a rolling pin on a floured work surface, roll the dough extremely thin (1 mm).
Using a fluted wheel or a knife, cut out diamonds, 4 inches | 10 cm long and 1 ½ to 2 inches | 4 to 5 cm wide. In the center of each diamond, make a slit lengthwise approximately 1 ¼ inches | 3 cm long.

4 ••· Preheat the fryer to 325°F to 340°F | 160°C to 170°C. Carefully lower the bugnes into the hot oil. Cook for approximately 2 minutes, turning over once during cooking. Use a skimmer (or slotted spoon) to remove from oil. Drain on paper towel, allow to cool completely and dust with confectioners' sugar.

Makes 30 to 40 financiers

Preparation: 20 minutes *Cooking time: 8 minutes* *Resting time: minimum of 12 hours*

Financiers

Financiers

6 ½ tbsp | 95 g butter
+ 1 ½ tbsp butter for moulds
1 ⅔ cups | 195 g confectioners' (icing) sugar
½ cup + 1 tbsp | 70 g cake flour
+ 2 ½ tbsp cake flour for moulds
⅔ cup | 65 g ground almonds (almond flour)
⅛ tsp (2 pinches) baking powder
6 egg whites
1 tsp vanilla extract

Equipment

Mini financier moulds, 1 x 2-inch | 2 ½ x 5-cm or individual financier moulds, 1 ¾ x 3 ½-inch | 4 ½ x 8 ½-cm, or barquette moulds, 3 ½ x 1 ½-inch | 9 x 4-cm
Pastry brush

Ideally, prepare the financier batter one day ahead.

1 ••• In a saucepan, melt the butter and allow to colour over medium heat until brown. As soon as you have a beurre noisette with a brown hazelnut colour, dip the bottom of the saucepan in cold water to immediately stop the butter from getting darker. Allow to cool to lukewarm.

2 ••• In a large bowl, mix the confectioners' sugar, flour and ground almonds. (You can also mix these ingredients in a food processor; pulse to obtain a fine powder.) Incorporate the baking powder. Add the egg whites little by little to avoid lumps, stirring in with a spatula. Pour in the vanilla and then the brown butter, which should be liquid and barely lukewarm. Stir to combine. Refrigerate batter for a minimum of 12 hours.

•••

3 ••• The following day, melt the 1 ½ tbsp of butter and using a pastry brush, butter the moulds. Refrigerate for 10 minutes to allow the butter to harden.
Preheat the oven to 410°F | 210°C | gas mark 6.
When the moulds have chilled, lightly dust with flour. Turn upside down and tap out any excess flour. Fill the moulds ¾ to the top with the financier batter.

4 ••• Place in oven and bake for 6 to 8 minutes until golden. Remove from oven and allow to cool slightly. Remove from the moulds and place on a rack to cool completely.

Chef's tips

You can keep the batter in the refrigerator for 2 to 3 days in a covered container; remove the desired amount to bake at any time.
Once baked, the financiers keep for 3 to 4 days; in this case, once they have cooled completely, store in an airtight container.

Makes 20 to 25 financiers
Preparation: 20 minutes *Cooking time: 8 minutes* *Resting time: minimum of 12 hours*

Financiers Pistache

Pistachio Financiers

9 tbsp | 125 g butter
+ 1 ½ tbsp butter for moulds
½ cup - 1 tbsp | 55 g confectioners' (icing) sugar
⅓ cup + 1 tbsp | 50 g cake flour
2 tbsp (15 g) ground pistachios (pistachio flour)
⅓ cup + 1 tbsp | 35 g ground almonds (almond flour)
⅕ tsp (3 pinches) baking powder
4 egg whites
1 ½ tbsp (25 g) pistachio paste

Equipment
Mini financier moulds, 1 x 2-inch | 2 ½ x 5-cm or individual financier moulds, 1 ¾ x 3 ½-inch | 4 ½ x 8 ½-cm, or barquette moulds, 3 ½ x 1 ½-inch | 9 x 4-cm
Pastry brush

Chef's tip
You can keep the batter in the refrigerator for 2 to 3 days in a covered container; remove the desired amount to bake at any time. Baked and cooled, the financiers keep for 3 to 4 days in an airtight container.

Prepare the financier batter one day ahead.

1 ••• In a saucepan, melt the butter over low heat.
In a large bowl, mix the confectioners' sugar, flour, ground pistachios, ground almonds and baking powder. Add the egg whites, little by little to avoid lumps, stirring in with a spatula.

2 ••• In a small bowl, thin the pistachio paste by mixing in a portion of the above preparation, and pour the whole mixture back into the large bowl. Add the melted butter (lukewarm) and stir to combine. Refrigerate batter for a minimum of 12 hours.

3 ••• The following day, preheat the oven to 410°F | 210°C | gas mark 6.
Melt the 1 ½ tbsp of butter and using a pastry brush, butter the moulds. Fill moulds ¾ to the top with the financier batter.

4 ••• Place in oven and bake for 6 to 8 minutes until golden. Remove from oven and allow to cool before removing from moulds.

Makes 24 individual madeleines or 60 mini madeleines
Preparation: 20 minutes *Cooking time: 10 minutes* *Resting time: minimum of 12 hours*

Madeleines

Madeleines

2 lemons, unwaxed
¾ cup + 1 tbsp | 160 g granulated sugar
1 ⅓ cups + 1 tbsp | 175 g cake flour
+ 2 ½ tbsp cake flour for moulds
2 tsp (10 g) baking powder
12 ½ tbsp | 180 g butter
+ 1 ½ tbsp butter for moulds
4 eggs
1 ⅔ tbsp (35 g) honey (mixed flower or acacia)

EQUIPMENT
Madeleine moulds
Grater
Pastry brush

Prepare the madeleine batter one day ahead.

1 ••• Using a grater, remove the zest from the lemons.
In a large bowl, mix the grated zest with the sugar.
In another bowl, sift together the flour and baking powder.
In a small saucepan, melt the butter over low heat.

2 ••• In another large bowl, place the eggs, the sugar and lemon zest mixture and the honey. Whip until pale and frothy. Fold in the flour and baking powder mixture. Add the melted butter and combine. Refrigerate batter for a minimum of 12 hours in a closed container.

•••

3 ••· The following day, melt the 1 ½ tbsp of butter, and using a pastry brush, butter the moulds. Refrigerate for 15 minutes to allow the butter to harden. Lightly dust with flour, turn upside down and tap out any excess. If you do not fill the moulds right away, keep them in the refrigerator.

4 ••· Preheat the oven to 390°F | 200°C | gas mark 6.
Fill moulds ¾ to the top with batter. Place in oven and bake mini madeleines for 5 to 6 minutes, and individual madeleines for 8 to 10 minutes. When golden, remove from oven and allow to cool slightly before removing from the moulds.

Chef's tips

Serve madeleines lukewarm. If you do not plan on serving them right after baking, allow to cool and store in an airtight container, so they will stay soft and moist.
While it is best to use nonstick moulds, it is still necessary to butter and flour them.

Makes 20 cannelés *Preparation: 30 minutes* *Cooking time: 1 hour* *Resting time: 24 hours*

Cannelés Bordelais

Bordeaux Cannelés

1 vanilla bean
2 cups + 2 tbsp | 500 ml whole milk
3 ½ tbsp | 50 g butter
+ 3 tbsp butter, softened for moulds
2 eggs + 2 egg yolks
2 cups | 240 g confectioners' (icing) sugar
1 ½ tbsp dark aged rum (rhum agricole if possible)
1 cup - 2 tbsp | 110 g cake flour
+ 2 ½ tbsp cake flour for moulds

EQUIPMENT

20 cannelé moulds, 2-inch | 5 ½-cm diameter

Prepare the cannelé batter one day ahead.

1 ••• With a sharp knife, slice the vanilla bean in half lengthwise. Using the tip, scrape the interior to remove the seeds. Pour the milk into a saucepan, add the vanilla pod and seeds and bring to a boil. Remove from heat, cover and allow to infuse for 1 hour. Remove the vanilla pod and allow to cool. Melt the butter and allow to cool. Sift the confectioners' sugar and flour in separate small bowls. In a large bowl, whisk together the eggs, egg yolks and the sifted confectioners' sugar. Continue to beat and add the following ingredients one after another, in this order: rum, melted butter, sifted flour and the vanilla-infused milk. Refrigerate the batter for a minimum of 12 hours.

2 ••• Coat the cannelé moulds with the softened butter and refrigerate for 15 minutes to allow the butter to harden. Lightly dust with flour, turn upside down and tap out any excess. If you do not fill moulds right away with batter, keep in the refrigerator. They must be filled just before being placed in a hot oven.

•••

3 ••· Preheat the oven to 350°F | 180°C | gas mark 4. Fill the chilled moulds to ⅕ inch | ½ cm below the rim. Place in oven and bake for 1 hour. It is possible that the cannelés will puff up during baking, simply prick the center with the tip of a knife. The exterior of the cannelés should turn very dark brown. As the French expression says, "when they're black, they're done." Immediately remove from the moulds and place onto a rack to cool. Serve at room temperature.

Chef's tips

Cannelés do not keep; you must serve them the day they are baked. However, you can prepare the batter in advance and keep it in the refrigerator for 2 to 3 days. Mix the batter before each use.

The type of mould is important. If possible, avoid using silicone moulds and instead, for the very best results, use copper.

Before using copper moulds for the very first time, use a pastry brush to coat the moulds with oil. Turn upside down and place on a rack. Bake for 20 minutes in a preheated oven at 480°F | 250°C | gas mark 9.

Buttering the moulds before each use thereafter will form a nonstick, protective film. Avoid washing them to have to repeat the above procedure. To clean, simply wipe moulds with a cloth while still hot.

Pain Perdu

French Toast

½ vanilla bean
1 ⅔ cups | 400 ml heavy (double) cream
4 egg yolks
½ cup - 2 tbsp | 80 g granulated sugar
1 round (mousseline) brioche, 8 inches | 20 cm high or 1 rectangular (Nanterre) brioche, 8 inches | 20 cm long
1 ½ tbsp butter for skillet

1 ••• With a sharp knife, slice the vanilla bean half lengthwise in two. Using the tip, scrape the interior to remove the seeds. Pour the cream into a saucepan, add the vanilla pod and seeds and bring to a simmer. Remove from heat, cover and allow to infuse for 1 hour until completely cool. Remove the vanilla pod.

2 ••• In a large bowl, whisk the egg yolks and sugar until slightly pale. Add the vanilla-infused cream, stirring in with a spatula.

3 ••• Cut the brioche into slices approximately ¾ inch | 2 cm thick. Remove the crusts.
Heat a knob of butter in a large skillet. Dip the brioche slices, tops and bottoms, in the above preparation and gently shake off any excess. Place in skillet. Cook for approximately 1 minute on each side until golden. Serve immediately.

Chef's tips

It is best to use slightly stale brioche (2 days old). After removing French toast from the skillet, drizzle with maple syrup.

Makes 10 apple turnovers

Preparation: 1 hour + basic recipe *Cooking time: 40 minutes* *Resting time: 2 hours*

Chaussons aux Pommes

Apple Turnovers

Puff pastry

17 ½ oz | 500 g dough: see basic recipe

2 ½ tbsp all-purpose flour for work surface

1 egg for finish

Apple compote

26 ½ oz | 750 g apples

(Jonagold or Boskoop if possible)

7 tbsp | 100 g butter

½ cup | 100 g granulated sugar

1 pinch of vanilla powder

(or a few drops of vanilla extract)

3 ⅓ tbsp (50 ml) water

½ lemon

Apple slices

2 apples (Granny Smith if possible)

Syrup

3 ⅓ tbsp (50 ml) water

¼ cup | 50 g granulated sugar

EQUIPMENT

Oval pastry cutter

Pastry brush

Puff pastry

1 ••• On a floured work surface, roll out the puff pastry dough to 1⁄10 inch | 2 mm thick.

Using the pastry cutter, cut out 10 ovals of dough. Place them on a baking sheet, overlapping. Refrigerate for 1 hour.

Apple compote

2 ••• Juice the lemon half. Using a vegetable peeler, peel the apples, then quarter and core. Cut into pieces 1⁄10-⅛ inch | 2-3 mm thick.

•••

Melt the butter in a saucepan and lightly brown the apples. Add the sugar, vanilla, water and lemon juice. Cover and cook over medium heat for approximately 10 minutes, until the apples are tender, translucent and start to break down.

To prevent a liquid compote, make this recipe with very little water. It is thus important to keep a close eye on the apples as they cook, and to completely cover the saucepan. Otherwise, while water evaporates, apples will get dark and stick to the bottom of the pan. If necessary, finish cooking the apples over low heat while stirring.

Remove from heat and allow to cool.

Apple slices

3 ••• Peel and core the apples, and cut into 8 slices. Cut each piece into 1/10-inch | 2-mm thick slices. Add to the cooled apple compote.

Apple filling

4 ••• Remove pastry from the refrigerator. Place an oval piece of dough on the work surface. Using a moistened pastry brush, brush water very lightly around the edge on one side of the dough. Place 2 spoonfuls of apple compote in the center and fold the dough back on itself to enclose the compote (in a half-circle pocket).

Seal the edges by pressing down lightly.

Repeat the above steps for all of the turnovers, and place upside down on a baking sheet lined with parchment paper.

5 ••· Beat the egg in a small bowl and brush the tops of the unbaked turnovers. Using the tip of a knife, draw half of a leaf on the surface of the dough. Refrigerate for 1 hour.
Preheat the oven to 350°F | 180°C | gas mark 4. Place sheet in oven and bake for approximately 40 minutes.

Syrup

6 ••· Meanwhile, prepare the syrup. Bring the water and sugar to a boil. Remove from heat and set aside.
As soon as you remove the turnovers from the oven, brush with syrup using a pastry brush.

Les Gâteaux de Goûter et Confiseries

Tea Cakes & Confections

For 8 to 10 people

Preparation: 1 ½ hours *Cooking time: 55 minutes* *Resting time: minimum of 12 hours*

Cake au Citron

Lemon Cake

Poached lemon slices

3 lemons, unwaxed

1 cup | 250 ml water

½ cup + 2 tbsp | 125 g granulated sugar

Lemon cake batter

5 tbsp | 75 g butter

+ 1 tbsp butter for loaf pan

1 ⅔ cups | 210 g all-purpose flour

+ 1 tbsp all-purpose flour for loaf pan

½ packet active dry yeast (1 tsp | 5 g)

1 lemon, unwaxed

1 ¼ cups | 250 g granulated sugar

3 eggs

½ cup - 1 tbsp | 110 ml heavy (double) cream

1 pinch of fleur de sel (or other coarse sea salt)

1 ⅔ tbsp (25 g) rum

Lemon syrup

½ cup | 125 ml water

½ cup + 2 tbsp | 120 g granulated sugar

¼ cup | 60 ml lemon juice

Lemon glaze

2 oz | 50 g lemon jelly

1 tbsp water

Equipment

Loaf pan, 10 x 3 x 3-inch | 25 x 8 x 8-cm

Grater

Poached lemon slices

1 ••• One day ahead, cut the lemons into thin 1⁄10-inch | 2-mm slices.
Bring the water and sugar to a simmer, and carefully add the lemon slices. Poach over very low heat for 20 minutes, without allowing the liquid to boil. Allow to cool. Transfer slices and liquid to a bowl or container and refrigerate for a minimum of 12 hours.
Set aside 6 attractive lemon slices to decorate the cake. Gently drain the remaining slices. Gather up to ½ cup | 120 g and cut each slice in half.

•••

Lemon cake batter

2 ••• Butter the loaf pan and line with a long rectangle of parchment paper to make unmoulding easier. Refrigerate for 10 minutes to allow the butter to harden. Remove from refrigerator and dust the interior with flour. Turn upside down and lightly tap out any excess flour.

3 ••• Place the 5 tbsp | 75 g of butter in a small saucepan and warm over low heat. As soon as it melts, remove from heat.
Sift the flour and yeast into a small bowl. Using a grater, remove the zest from the lemon. Toss the zest with the sugar in a large bowl. Add the eggs one at a time, while whisking together. Continue to whisk and add the cream, salt and rum. Using a wooden or rubber spatula, fold in the flour and yeast mixture, halved lemon slices and melted butter (lukewarm).

4 ••• Preheat the oven to 410°F | 210°C | gas mark 6.
Fill the loaf pan with batter to ¾ inch | 2 cm below the rim. Place in oven and bake for 10 minutes. Remove from oven, and using a knife, make a slit lengthwise in the crust that has formed on top of the cake. Immediately return cake to the oven and lower the temperature to 350°F | 180°C | gas mark 4. Bake for 45 minutes. Check to see if the cake is done by inserting the tip of a knife into the center. When the cake is ready, the knife should come out clean, dry and free of crumbs.

Lemon syrup

5 ••• While the cake is baking, prepare the syrup. Bring the water, sugar and lemon juice to a boil. Remove from heat.

6 ••• Place a cooling rack on a rimmed baking sheet. When the cake is done, removed from the mould and place on the rack. Bring the syrup to a simmer. Using a ladle, pour syrup over cake and allow to soak. Gather syrup from baking sheet and pour over cake. Repeat twice. Allow to cool. Decorate the cake with the poached lemon slices.

Lemon glaze

7 ••• In a saucepan, stir together the lemon jelly and water. Lightly heat without bringing to a boil (to approximately 122°F to 140°F | 50°C to 60°C), until the mixture is thick enough to coat the back of a spoon. Coat cake with glaze.

Chef's tip

Keep the cake in the refrigerator, sealed in plastic wrap or in an airtight container.
You can serve the cake directly from the refrigerator, chilled and refreshing, or you can remove it an hour before serving to soften.

For 8 to 10 people
Preparation: 1 ½ hours *Cooking time: 55 minutes* *Resting time: minimum of 12 hours*

Cake Chocolat à l'Orange

Chocolate Orange Cake

Poached orange slices
1 orange
¾ cup + 2 tbsp | 200 ml water
½ cup | 100 g granulated sugar

Chocolate cake batter
½ cup | 75 g golden seedless raisins (sultanas)
10 ½ tbsp | 150 g butter
+ 1 tbsp butter for loaf pan
1 cup - 1 tbsp | 120 g all-purpose flour
+ 1 tbsp all-purpose flour for loaf pan
⅓ cup | 30 g unsweetened cocoa powder
½ packet active dry yeast (1 tsp | 5 g)
¾ cup | 150 g granulated sugar
3 eggs
1 ¼ cups | 210 g candied orange, diced

Orange syrup
⅔ cup - 1 tbsp | 150 ml orange juice
½ cup + 2 tbsp | 120 g granulated sugar
⅓ cup | 80 ml Grand Marnier

Orange glaze
2 oz | 50 g orange jelly
1 tbsp water

EQUIPMENT
Loaf pan, 10 x 3 x 3-inch | 25 x 8 x 8-cm

POACHED ORANGE SLICES

1 ••• One day ahead, cut the orange into thin ⅒-inch | 2-mm slices. Bring the water and sugar to a simmer, and carefully add the orange slices. Poach over very low heat for 30 minutes without allowing the liquid to boil. Allow to cool. Gently drain the orange slices and keep in the refrigerator.

•••

Chocolate cake batter

2 ••· Also one day ahead, place the raisins in a bowl. Top with enough hot water to cover the raisins by ⅓ inch | 1 cm. Cover the bowl with plastic wrap and allow the raisins to soak and swell for a minimum of 12 hours at room temperature. Gently drain.

3 ••· The following day, butter the loaf pan and line with a long rectangle of parchment paper to make unmoulding easier. Refrigerate for 10 minutes to allow the butter to harden. Remove from refrigerator and dust the interior with flour. Turn upside down and lightly tap out any excess flour.

4 ••· Bring the butter and eggs to room temperature.
In a large bowl, sift together the cocoa powder, flour and yeast.
In another bowl, work the butter until creamy. Add the sugar and whisk vigorously. Continue to whip and incorporate the eggs one at a time. Using a wooden or rubber spatula, fold in the cocoa mixture. Add the drained raisins and diced candied orange.

5 ••· Preheat the oven to 425°F | 220°C | gas mark 7.
Fill the loaf pan with batter to ¾ inch | 2 cm below the rim. Place in oven and bake for 10 minutes. Remove from oven, and using a knife, make a slit lengthwise in the crust that has formed on top of the cake. Immediately return cake to the oven and lower the temperature to 350°F | 180°C | gas mark 4. Bake for 40 to 45 minutes. Check to see if the cake is done by inserting the tip of a knife into the center. When the cake is ready, the knife should come out clean, dry and free of crumbs.

Orange syrup

6 ••• While the cake is baking, prepare the syrup. Bring orange juice and sugar to a boil.
Remove from heat and pour in the Grand Marnier.

7 ••• Place a cooling rack on a rimmed baking sheet. When the cake is done, remove from the mould and place on the rack. Bring the syrup to a simmer. Using a ladle, pour syrup over cake and allow to soak. Gather syrup from baking sheet and pour over cake. Repeat twice. Allow to cool. Decorate the top of the cake with the poached orange slices.

Orange glaze

8 ••• In a saucepan, stir together the orange jelly and water. Lightly heat without bringing to a boil (to approximately 122°F to 140°F | 50°C to 60°C), until the mixture is thick enough to coat the back of a spoon.
Coat cake with glaze.

For 8 to 10 people

Preparation: 1 ½ hours *Cooking time: 55 minutes* *Resting time: 12 hours + 24 hours*

Pain d'Épices

Gingerbread

⅔ cup | 150 ml water
⅓ oz | 10 g star anise or wild anise
5 tbsp | 75 g butter
+ 1 ½ tbsp butter for loaf pan
½ cup | 100 g granulated sugar
⅓ cup | 100 g chestnut honey
1 orange, unwaxed
1 lemon, unwaxed
1 cup | 110 g rye flour
1 cup - 2 tbsp | 115 g all-purpose flour
+ 2 ½ tbsp all-purpose flour for loaf pan
½ packet active dry yeast (1 tsp | 5 g)
2 tsp (5 g) ground cinnamon
1 tsp (3 g) ground quatre épices (blend of ground pepper, cloves, nutmeg, ginger)
2 tbsp (30 g) candied orange, diced

Equipment

Loaf pan, 10 x 3 x 3-inch | 25 x 8 x 8-cm
Grater

1 ••• Ideally, begin recipe one day ahead so that the following liquid has time to cool completely.
In a saucepan, bring the water, star anise, butter, sugar and honey to a boil. Remove from heat, cover and allow to infuse for 2 hours. Strain with a fine mesh sieve and discard the solids. Allow to cool at room temperature overnight.

2 ••• The following day, butter the loaf pan and line with a long rectangle of parchment paper to make unmoulding easier. Refrigerate for 10 minutes to allow the butter to harden. Remove from refrigerator and dust the interior with flour. Turn upside down and lightly tap out any excess flour.

•••

3 ••· Using a grater, remove the zest from the orange and lemon.
In a large bowl, sift together the flours, yeast, cinnamon and quatre épices. Add the citrus zest and diced candied orange.
Pour the cold, infused liquid over the dry mixture in several parts, stirring with a wooden spatula to avoid lumps (as you would for crêpe batter).

4 ••· Preheat the oven to 410°F | 210°C | gas mark 6.
Fill the loaf pan with gingerbread batter to ¾ inch | 2 cm below the rim. Place in oven and bake for 10 minutes. Remove from oven, and using a knife, make a slit lengthwise in the crust that has formed on top of the cake. Immediately return cake to the oven and lower the temperature to 350°F | 180°C | gas mark 4. Bake for 45 minutes. Check to see if the cake is done by inserting the tip of a knife into the center. When the cake is ready, the knife should come out clean, dry and free of crumbs.

5 ••· Remove from oven and allow to cool for 5 minutes.
Remove from the mould and place on a wire rack to cool completely.

Chef's tip

Once the gingerbread is cool, wrap in plastic wrap and allow to dry out slightly at room temperature for 24 hours before tasting.

L

Makes 20 crêpes

Preparation: 20 minutes *Cooking time: 3 minutes per crêpe* *Resting time: minimum of 1 hour*

Crêpes

Crêpes

1 orange, unwaxed
1 ⅓ cups | 165 g cake flour
3 tbsp (40 g) granulated sugar
4 eggs
2 cups + 2 tbsp | 500 ml whole milk
3 tbsp | 40 g butter
+ 1 ½ tbsp butter for skillet

1 tbsp oil
1 tbsp rum (optional)
1 tbsp Cointreau or Grand Marnier (optional)

EQUIPMENT

Grater

1 ••· Using a grater, remove the zest from the orange.
Sift the flour into a large bowl. Add the sugar, grated orange zest and eggs. Gradually add the milk while whisking constantly to obtain a smooth batter without lumps. In a small saucepan, slowly melt the butter. Add to batter, along with the oil and alcohols if desired.
Allow the batter to rest at room temperature for a minimum of 1 hour.

2 ••· Lightly butter the surface of a skillet (preferably nonstick) with paper towel. Using a ladle, pour enough batter to coat the surface of the hot pan, and tilt the pan to form a thin, even layer. Cook on one side over low heat until the batter sets (barely 1 minute).
Flip crêpe over and cook the other side until lightly golden.

••·

As you cook the crêpes, stack one on top of another to keep them soft and moist. If you have two pans, preparation is faster; while one crêpe is cooking, you can fill the other.

3 ••• Sprinkle crêpes with sugar or top with fruit jam (low in sugar), melted chocolate or hazelnut spread. "Personally, I like them with lemon, lightly sprinkled with sugar."

Chef's tips

Prepare the crêpe batter 2 hours in advance.
If there are lumps, blend as briefly as possible simply to get rid of them, but without making the batter frothy.
If you would like to cook the crêpes in advance, stack one on top of another as you go along, so they stay soft and moist. Keep at room temperature.

Makes 10 waffles

Preparation: 15 minutes *Cooking time: 3 minutes per waffle* *Resting time: 1 hour*

Gaufres Maison

Waffles

½ cup + 1 ½ tbsp | 75 g cake flour
½ cup | 125 ml whole milk
+ ⅓ cup | 75 ml whole milk
1 ½ tbsp (20 g) granulated sugar
1 pinch of salt
2 tbsp | 30 g butter
3 eggs

¼ cup | 50 ml crème fraîche (or sour cream)
1 tbsp orange flower water

Confectioners' (icing) sugar for dusting

EQUIPMENT
Waffle iron
Pastry brush

1 ••· Sift the flour. In a saucepan, bring the ½ cup | 125 ml of whole milk, sugar, salt and butter to a boil. Remove from heat. Incorporate the flour by mixing energetically with a spatula until homogenous.
Return the saucepan to low heat and stir vigorously for 1 minute to pull out the moisture from the batter, so that it forms a mass and pulls away from the sides of the pan.

2 ••· Transfer batter to a large bowl and allow to cool. Add the eggs one at a time, carefully incorporating each into the batter with a spatula.

3 ••· Add the crème fraîche, the ⅓ cup | 75 ml of whole milk and the orange flower water. Stir together and allow to rest at room temperature for 1 hour.

••·

4 ••• Preheat the waffle iron. Oil very lightly with a pastry brush.
Pour in enough batter for one waffle. Cook for approximately 3 to 4 minutes until golden.
Dust with confectioners' sugar.

Chef's tip

For me, when it comes to eating waffles with my hands, I adore them lightly covered in sweetened whipped cream and with a touch of strawberry jam (with not too much sugar added). If you serve the waffles warm on a plate, accompany with sweetened whipped cream and a strawberry or raspberry coulis. The coulis is not as sweet as the jam, so it will have a more fruity flavour.

For 8 people   Preparation: 40 minutes   Cooking time: 25 minutes

Gâteau Moelleux au Chocolat

Soft Chocolate cake

10 ½ tbsp | 150 g butter
+ 1 ½ tbsp butter for cake pan
¼ cup | 35 g cake flour
+ 2 ½ tbsp cake flour for cake pan
5 oz | 150 g chocolate (minimum 70% cacao solids)
1 tbsp unsweetened cocoa powder
1 egg + 4 egg yolks + 7 egg whites
¾ cup | 150 g granulated sugar

Equipment

Round cake pan with straight or sloping sides, 9-inch | 22 ½-cm diameter

1 ••• Butter the cake pan and refrigerate for 5 minutes to allow the butter to set. Remove from refrigerator and dust the interior with flour. Turn upside down and lightly tap out any excess flour. Keep in the refrigerator. Using a knife, chop the chocolate on a cutting board. Place in a heatproof bowl set over a pan of gently simmering water. Add the butter and melt together over very low heat, stirring with a spatula. Remove from heat. Sift together the flour and cocoa powder, and set aside.

2 ••• Preheat the oven to 350°F | 180°C | gas mark 4.
In a large mixing bowl, placed over a pan of gently simmering water, whisk together (as you would for génoise) the egg, egg yolks and half of the sugar (about ⅓ cup | 75 g), until the mixture thickens. Remove from heat and set aside. Immediately whisk the egg whites to a foam in another large clean, dry bowl. Once they are white and frothy, incorporate the remaining half of sugar (about ⅓ cup | 75 g), while continuing to whisk for another minute.

•••

3 ••• Delicately fold a third of the egg and sugar mixture into the melted chocolate and butter. Pour the entire mixture back over the remaining ⅔ of the eggs and sugar, mixing gently.

Delicately fold a third of the whipped egg whites, along with the sifted flour and cocoa powder, into the above mixture. Pour this new mixture then back over the remaining ⅔ of whipped egg whites. Combine all together until smooth, being careful not to overmix.

4 ••• Pour batter into the cake pan. Place in oven and lower the temperature to 340°F | 170°C | gas mark 3. Bake for 25 minutes. Remove from oven and allow to cool for 30 minutes before removing from the mould.

Chef's tip

Keep cake at room temperature and serve within 24 hours.

For 8 people

Preparation: 1 hour + base recipe *Cooking time: approximately 45 minutes* *Resting time: 1 hour*

Flan patissier

Custard Tart

Shortcrust pastry for tart shell

See base recipe

2 ½ tbsp all-purpose flour for work surface

1 ½ tbsp butter for tart pan

Custard filling

2 vanilla beans

2 cups + 2 tbsp | 500 ml whole milk

1 ⅓ cups | 325 ml heavy (double) cream

2 eggs + 2 egg yolks

1 cup + 1 tbsp | 210 g granulated sugar

⅔ cup | 85 g cornstarch (cornflour)

2 tbsp | 25 g butter

EQUIPMENT

Tart pan, 9-inch | 22 ½-cm diameter, 1 ¼ inches | 3 cm high

SHORTCRUST PASTRY FOR TART SHELL

1 ••• Prepare the shortcrust pastry dough (see base recipe). On a floured work surface, roll out the dough to a thickness of $\frac{1}{10}$ inch | 2 mm. Butter the tart pan and gently press the dough into the pan, working up the sides. Trim any excess dough that hangs over the edges. Refrigerate for 1 hour.

CUSTARD FILLING

2 ••• With a sharp knife, slice the vanilla beans in half lengthwise. Using the tip, scrape the interior to remove the seeds. Pour the milk and cream into a saucepan and add the vanilla pods and seeds. Bring to a simmer. Remove from heat, cover and let infuse for 15 minutes. Remove the vanilla pods and set aside.

•••

3 ••• Preheat the oven to 340°F | 170°C | gas mark 3.
Using a fork, prick the surface of the dough to keep from puffing up during baking. Fit a round piece of parchment paper over the dough, carefully pressing into the corners and working up the sides so it will stay in place in the oven. Place dried beans or pie weights on top, spreading them out in an even layer. Bake for approximately 20 minutes until the crust is lightly coloured.
Remove from oven and allow to cool.
Remove pie weights and parchment paper.

4 ••• In a large bowl, whisk the eggs, egg yolks and sugar until slightly pale. Add the cornstarch.
In a saucepan, bring the vanilla-infused milk and cream to a simmer. Pour a third of the hot liquid over the egg, sugar and cornstarch mixture (to temper the eggs). Whisk together and then pour back into the saucepan with the other ⅔ of milk and cream. Bring to a boil while continuing to stir with the whisk, making sure to scrape down the sides of the pan with a spatula.
Remove from heat, pour the custard into a large bowl and allow to cool slightly for approximately 10 minutes.

5 ••• Meanwhile, preheat the oven again to 340°F | 170°C | gas mark 3.
When the custard is still hot but not scalding, add the butter, stirring until homogenous. Pour the custard into the pre-baked tart shell.
Place in oven and bake for approximately 45 minutes.

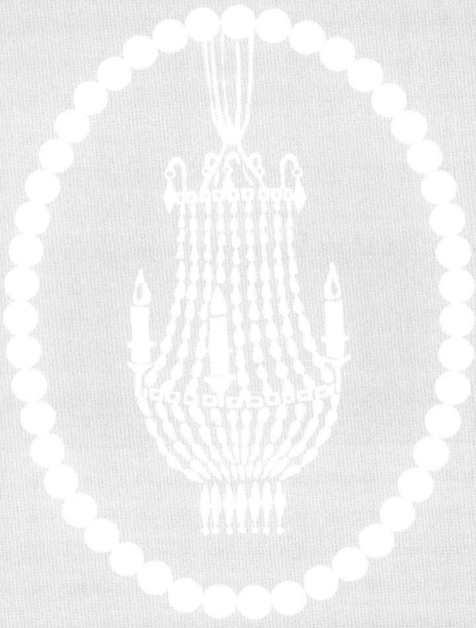

For 8 people Preparation: 15 minutes Cooking time: 40 minutes

Clafoutis aux Cerises

Cherry Clafoutis

1 lemon, unwaxed
¾ cup + 2 tbsp | 175 g granulated sugar
+ 1 ½ tbsp granulated sugar for tart pan
1 pinch of salt
⅓ cup | 50 g cornstarch (cornflour)
⅓ cup | 50 g cake flour
3 eggs + 2 egg yolks
1 ¼ cups | 300 ml whole milk
1 ¼ cups | 300 ml heavy (double) cream
17 ½ oz | 500 g cherries
1 ½ tbsp butter for tart pan

Equipment

Tart pan, 10-inch | 25-cm diameter, 1 ¼ inches | 3 cm high
Grater
Pastry brush

1 ••• Using a grater, zest the lemon.
In a bowl, whisk together the sugar and lemon zest. Incorporate the salt, cornstarch and flour. Add the eggs and egg yolks, and whisk all together. Add the milk and cream, and mix to combine.

2 ••• Pit the cherries. Preheat the oven to 340°F | 170°C | gas mark 3.
Melt the butter. Using a pastry brush, butter the tart pan and sprinkle with sugar. Arrange the cherries in the pan. Pour in the batter and bake for approximately 40 minutes.

Chef's tip

Using whole cherries (with pits) will give your clafoutis more flavour and the cherries will lose less water (avoiding a soggy clafoutis). You can also prepare the clafoutis in a shortcrust pastry shell, prebaked at 340°F | 170°C | gas mark 3 for approx. 20 minutes until lightly coloured. Fill with cherries and clafoutis batter. The cooking time is then identical as above.

For 8 people *Preparation: 1 ½ hours* *Cooking time: 45 minutes*

Soft Orange Cake

Gâteau moelleux à l'orange

Poached orange slices

1 orange, unwaxed
¾ cup + 2 tbsp | 200 ml water
½ cup | 100 g granulated sugar

Cake batter

1 cup | 225 g butter
+ 1 ½ tbsp butter for cake pan
1 ⅓ cups + 1 tbsp | 175 g all-purpose flour
+ 2 ½ tbsp all-purpose flour for cake pan
3 eggs
3 oranges, unwaxed
1 cup + 2 tbsp | 225 g granulated sugar
1 packet active dry yeast (2 tsp | 11 g)

Orange syrup

½ cup | 90 g granulated sugar
¾ cup + 1 tbsp | 200 ml orange juice

Orange glaze

3 ½ oz | 100 g orange jelly
2 tbsp water

EQUIPMENT

Round cake pan with sloping sides, 9-inch | 22-cm diameter
Grater

POACHED ORANGE SLICES

1 ••• Wash the orange and cut into thin ⅒-inch | 2-mm slices. Bring the water and sugar to a simmer, and carefully add the orange slices. Keep over very low heat for 20 minutes, without allowing the liquid to boil. Drain the slices and allow to cool.

CAKE BATTER

2 ••• Butter the cake pan and line the bottom with a round piece of parchment paper to make unmoulding easier. Refrigerate for 10 minutes to allow the butter to harden. Remove from refrigerator and dust the interior with flour. Turn upside down and lightly tap out excess flour. •••

3 ••· Bring the eggs to room temperature.
Using a grater, zest the oranges. Combine the grated zest with the sugar. Juice the oranges and set aside.

4 ••· Put the butter in a large heatproof bowl set over a pan of simmering water or in the microwave to soften until creamy. Add the following ingredients, one after another, making sure to mix well after each addition: sugar and zest mixture, eggs at room temperature, flour, yeast and the juice from the oranges.
Preheat the oven to 350°F | 180°C | gas mark 4.
Fill the cake pan with batter to ¾ inch | 2 cm below the rim. Place in oven and bake for 45 minutes.

Orange syrup

5 ••· While the cake is baking, prepare the syrup. Bring sugar and orange juice to a boil. Remove from heat.

6 ••· Place a cooling rack on a rimmed baking sheet. When the cake is done, remove from the mould and place on the rack. Bring the syrup to a simmer. Using a ladle, pour syrup over cake and allow to soak. Gather syrup from baking sheet and pour over cake. Repeat twice. Allow to cool. Decorate the top of the cake with the poached orange slices.

Orange glaze

7 ••· In a saucepan, stir together the orange jelly and water. Lightly heat without bringing to a boil (to approximately 122°F to 140°F | 50°C to 60°C), until the mixture is thick enough to coat the back of a spoon.
Coat cake with glaze.
Allow to cool and serve cake at room temperature.

Makes 65 marshmallow squares, 1 ¼ inches | 3 cm thick
Preparation: 1 hour (in 2 parts) *Cooking time: 15 minutes* *Resting time: 12 to 24 hours*

Guimauve Fraise & Fleur d'Oranger

Strawberry & Orange Flower Marshmallows

Marshmallow

12 gelatin sheets (3 tbsp | 21 g powdered gelatin)
⅔ cup | 150 ml water
2 ½ cups | 500 g granulated sugar
+ 2 tbsp (25 g) granulated sugar
¼ cup | 75 g glucose syrup (or corn syrup)
6 egg whites
½ cup | 100 g strawberry pulp
5 tbsp orange flower water

Presentation

¾ cup | 100 g confectioners' (icing) sugar
⅔ cup | 100 g potato starch

Equipment

Candy thermometer (required)
10-inch | 25-cm square ring mould
or baking sheet with 1 ¼-inch | 3-cm rim

1 ••• Cut parchment paper to line the surface of a baking sheet and place the square mould on top.
If you do not have a square mould, cut a piece of aluminum foil 20 inches | 50 cm long. Fold several times lengthwise to create a strip 20 x 1 ¼-inch | 50 x 3-cm.
Fold this strip in half to obtain a right angle with two 10-inch | 25-cm long sides. Place on the rimmed baking sheet, and using 2 sides of the sheet, form a square in the corner. By doing this, you will have created a 10 x 10-inch | 25 x 25-cm frame.

2 ••• Place the gelatin sheets in a small bowl of very cold water. Allow to soften for 10 minutes.
Drain the gelatin sheets, squeezing hard to remove all excess liquid and set aside.
•••

Put the ⅔ cup | 150 ml of water, granulated sugar and glucose syrup in a saucepan. Bring mixture to 270°F | 130°C on the candy thermometer. When the sugar reaches 250°F | 120°C, start to beat the egg whites in a large clean, dry bowl. Once they are white and frothy, add the 2 tbsp (25 g) of granulated sugar and whip. The egg whites and cooked sugar must be ready at the same time. Incorporate the cooked sugar little by little into the whipped egg whites, continuing to whip to obtain a meringue.

3 ••• Add the well-drained gelatin sheets to the hot meringue. Combine to melt the gelatin. Using a wooden spoon or rubber spatula, delicately fold in the strawberry pulp and the orange flower water.

4 ••• Pour the marshmallow into the square mould, to a thickness of 1 ¼ inches | 3 cm. Allow to cool completely and harden overnight in a cool place (54°F to 61°F | 12°C to 16°C). You can also cover with plastic wrap and place in the refrigerator.

5 ••• The following day, prepare a mixture of confectioners' sugar and potato starch to use for cutting and coating the marshmallows. Sprinkle some over the work surface.

Slide the tip of a knife around the inside of the mould to loosen the set marshmallow. Remove from the mould and place on the work surface.

For marshmallow squares, use a knife dipped in hot water, wiped clean before each cut.

Slice strips 1 ¼ inches | 3 cm thick and cut again in the opposite direction to form 1 ¼ x 1 ¼-inch | 3 x 3-cm squares.

Roll the cut marshmallows in the confectioners' sugar and potato starch mixture to coat, shake off any excess and allow to dry uncovered for 6 hours.

Chef's tip

Marshmallows can be eaten as soon as they are ready, or kept for 5 to 6 days, stored in an airtight container, preferably in the refrigerator.

Makes about 1 lb | 500 g of caramel or 50 small caramel squares
Preparation: 20 minutes   Cooking time: 10 to 15 minutes   Resting time: 4 to 6 hours

Caramels Mous au Chocolat

Soft Chocolate Caramels

4 oz | 120 g chocolate (70% cacao solids)
⅓ cup | 75 ml water
1 cup - 1 tbsp | 190 g granulated sugar
⅓ cup | 140 g glucose syrup (or corn syrup)
¾ cup + 1 tbsp | 200 ml heavy (double) cream
1 ½ tbsp | 20 g butter

Equipment
Candy thermometer
Square ring mould or round tart ring,
⅓-¾ inch | 1-2 cm thick

1 ••• Using a knife, chop the chocolate on a cutting board, and set aside in a large bowl.
In a saucepan, bring the water and sugar to a boil. Add the glucose syrup and cook over medium heat for approximately 10 to 15 minutes.
Meanwhile, in another saucepan, bring the cream to a simmer. Remove from heat and set aside.

2 ••• Once the sugar has a golden caramel colour, remove from heat. Stir in the butter. Slowly add the hot cream, pouring in a thin stream and stirring with a wooden spoon. Be very careful as you do not want the caramel to bubble and spurt.
Cook this caramel again to 240°F | 115°C on the candy thermometer, while stirring with a wooden spatula. Pour caramel over the chopped chocolate and stir until just combined.

•••

3 ••• Place the square mould or round tart ring on a baking sheet lined with parchment paper and pour in the caramel.

4 ••• Allow to cool for 4 to 6 hours. Cut the caramel into small squares or rectangles and wrap each one in cellophane paper. Store in a cool, dry place.

Variations

Soft milk chocolate caramel: cook the caramel the second time to 243°F | 117°C instead of 240°F | 115°C.

Soft vanilla and white chocolate caramel: cook the caramel the first time to 325°F | 160°C for a light coloured caramel, and the second time to 250°F | 120°C.

Makes 40 to 50 truffles *Preparation: 1 hour* *Resting time: 2 hours*

Truffes au Chocolat

Chocolate Truffles

4 ½ tbsp | 65 g butter
9 oz | 250 g dark chocolate (70% cacao solids)
⅔ cup | 150 ml heavy (double) cream
1 ½ tbsp (20 g) granulated sugar
1 cup + 3 tbsp | 100 g unsweetened cocoa powder

Equipment

Piping bag fitted with a ½-inch | 10-mm plain tip

1 ••• Cut the butter into small pieces. Place in a heatproof bowl set over a pan of gently simmering water or in the microwave, and soften until creamy without allowing it to melt. Remove from heat and whisk until homogenous.

2 ••• Using a knife, finely chop the chocolate on a cutting board, and place in a large bowl.
In a saucepan, bring the cream and sugar to a boil. Pour this hot liquid over the chopped chocolate in 3 parts, making sure to combine well after each addition. Add the softened butter and combine until homogenous.

3 ••• Pour the ganache into a baking dish. Cover with plastic wrap and refrigerate for 1 hour to cool completely. Remove from refrigerator and leave to rest at room temperature for 30 minutes, to give it a smooth yet firm texture.

4 ••• Transfer ganache to the piping bag fitted with a plain tip. Pipe small rounds on a baking sheet lined with parchment paper. Place sheet in the refrigerator for 30 minutes for the truffles to become firm.
Put cocoa powder in a small bowl or dish. Roll truffles in cocoa powder to coat. Store truffles in an airtight container in the refrigerator.

Les Petits Biscuits

Biscuits & Cookies

Makes 60 small shortbread biscuits *Preparation: 30 minutes* *Cooking time: 15 to 20 minutes*

Sablés Viennois

Viennese Shortbread

½ cup + 5 ½ tbsp | 190 g butter
+ 1 ½ tbsp butter for baking sheet
1 pinch of fleur de sel (or other coarse sea salt)
⅔ cup | 75 g confectioners' (icing) sugar
+ extra confectioners' (icing) sugar for dusting
1 pinch of powdered vanilla
(or a few drops of vanilla extract)
1 egg white
1 ¾ cups | 225 g cake flour

Equipment

Piping bag fitted with a ⅙-inch | 4-mm star tip

1 ••• Cut the butter into small pieces. Put butter and fleur de sel in a heatproof bowl set over a pan of gently simmering water. Using a wooden spoon, soften until creamy. Remove from heat and whisk until homogenous.
Add the following ingredients, one after another, making sure to mix well after each addition: confectioners' sugar, powdered vanilla and the egg white. Whisk together.

2 ••• Preheat the oven to 300°F | 150°C | gas mark 2.
Sift the flour and add to the mixture, stirring with a wooden spoon until homogenous.

3 ••• Immediately transfer batter to the piping bag fitted with a star tip.
Butter a baking sheet or line with parchment paper, and pipe ribbons in the shape of the letter Z, 1 ¼ x 1 ½-inch | 3 x 4-cm.
Place sheet in oven and bake for 15 to 20 minutes, until the shortbread biscuits are golden.
Allow to cool completely.
Dust lightly with confectioners' sugar.

Chef's tip
Store shortbread biscuits in an airtight container in a cool, dry place.

Makes 65 small or 24 large shortbread biscuits
Preparation: 30 minutes   Cooking time: 15 minutes
Resting time: minimum of 2 hours, ideally 12 hours

Sablés Noix de Coco

Coconut Shortbread

1 ½ cups | 325 g butter
1 pinch of fleur de sel (or other coarse sea salt)
1 ¼ cups | 150 g confectioners' (icing) sugar
¾ cup | 75 g ground almonds (almond flour)
½ cup + 2 tbsp | 75 g ground coconut (coconut flour)
1 egg
2 ⅔ cups | 325 g cake flour
+ 2 ½ tbsp cake flour for work surface

Equipment
Rolling pin
Round pastry cutter, 1 ½-2 inch | 4-5 cm diameter for small biscuits, 3-4 inch | 8-10 cm for large biscuits

1 ••• Sift the confectioners' sugar.
Cut the butter into small pieces and put in a large bowl. Work the butter to homogenize. Add the following ingredients, one after another, making sure to fully incorporate after each addition: fleur de sel, sifted confectioners' sugar, ground almonds, ground coconut, egg and lastly, the flour. This can also be done using a stand mixer fitted with the paddle attachment. Mix the ingredients just so the dough comes together; do not overwork. This will give the biscuits their desired crumbly texture.

2 ••• Form the dough into a ball and wrap in plastic wrap. Refrigerate for several hours (minimum of 2 hours) before using. It is better to prepare the dough one day ahead; it will be easier to roll out.

•••

3 ••• Preheat the oven to 325°F | 160°C | gas mark 3.
Using a rolling pin on a floured work surface, roll out the dough until it is approximately 1⁄10 inch | 2 mm thick.
Using the pastry cutter, cut out as many disks as you can, and place in rows on a baking sheet lined with parchment paper.

4 ••• Place sheet in oven and bake for approximately 15 minutes until golden.
Allow shortbread to cool completely.

Chef's tip
Store shortbread biscuits in an airtight container.

Makes 50 biscuits *Preparation: 20 minutes* *Cooking time: 10 to 12 minutes*

Langues de Chat

Cat's Tongues

9 tbsp | 125 g butter
1 ⅓ cups | 160 g confectioners' (icing) sugar
1 packet of vanilla sugar
(or 2 tsp sugar + 1 tsp vanilla extract)

2 egg whites
1 ¼ cups | 160 g cake flour

Equipment
Piping bag fitted with a ⅕-inch | 5-mm plain tip

1 ••• Cut the butter into small pieces and put in a heatproof bowl set over a pan of gently simmering water. Using a wooden spoon, soften the butter until creamy. Remove from heat and whisk until homogenous.
Add the following ingredients, one after another, making sure to mix well after each addition: confectioners' sugar, vanilla sugar and the egg whites. Whisk together.

2 ••• Sift the flour and add to the mixture, stirring with a wooden spoon until homogenous.

3 ••• Preheat the oven to 325°F | 160°C | gas mark 3.
Transfer the batter to the piping bag fitted with a plain tip. Pipe 2 ⅓-inch | 6-cm long strips onto a baking sheet lined with parchment paper. Leave space between each one, as they will spread during baking.

•••

4 ••• Place sheet in oven and bake for 10 to 12 minutes until golden.
Allow the biscuits to cool to room temperature on the baking sheet before removing with a spatula.
When they have cooled completely, store in an airtight container.

Variations

You can dip the biscuits in dark, milk or white chocolate, or coloured white chocolate using food colouring, and place on parchment paper to dry.

Melted, tempered chocolate can be quite technical. Here is a simple method: using a knife, chop chocolate on a cutting board. Place in a heatproof bowl set over a pan of gently simmering water to melt. Pour ¾ of this chocolate mass onto a clean, dry work surface. Using an offset stainless steel spatula, spread melted chocolate out, gather together again and work back and forth until it starts to thicken. Return to bowl with remaining ¼ of melted chocolate and mix well to homogenize. The tempered chocolate is used at 86°F to 88°F | 30°C to 31°C. Too hot or too cold and it will bloom (turn white) when cooled.

Once the biscuits are dipped in this tempered chocolate, allow to set and store in an airtight container.

Chef's tip

Plain biscuits are an excellent accompaniment to chocolate mousse or fruit salad.

Makes 50 macaroons
Preparation: 20 minutes *Cooking time: 15 minutes* *Resting time: minimum of 12 hours*

Rochers Noix de Coco

Coconut Macaroons

⅓ cup + 1 tbsp | 100 ml whole milk
1 cup + 2 tbsp | 225 g granulated sugar
1 ¾ cups + 2 tbsp | 275 g ground coconut (coconut flour)
2 ½ tbsp (20 g) cake flour
4 eggs

Equipment

Piping bag fitted with a ½-inch | 14-mm plain tip

1 ••• Prepare the batter one day ahead.
In a saucepan, warm the milk. Do not allow it to boil. Remove from heat. Add the sugar and ground coconut. Cover and allow to steep for 1 hour, allowing the coconut to soak in the milk and the mixture to cool down.

2 ••• Fold in the flour and eggs with a spatula.
Refrigerate for a minimum of 12 hours, to allow the coconut to steep completely.

3 ••• The following day, preheat the oven to 350°F | 180°C | gas mark 4.
Transfer batter to the piping bag fitted with a plain tip. Pipe small mounds onto a baking sheet lined with parchment paper. You can also shape macaroons using a spoon: dip a spoon in water and scoop out the amount of batter needed; slide off spoon with your index finger. Dip fingers in water and pinch the dough with 4 fingers to shape like small rocks (rochers).

4 ••• Place sheet in oven and bake for approximately 15 minutes until macaroons are lightly coloured.
Allow to cool completely and store in an airtight container.

Makes 30 biscuits *Preparation: 20 minutes* *Cooking time: 12 to 15 minutes*

Abricotines

Abricotines

1 ⅓ cups + 1 tbsp | 170 g confectioners' (icing) sugar + ¼ cup | 30 g confectioners' (icing) sugar for dusting
2 ¼ cups | 215 g ground almonds (almond flour)
¼ cup | 35 g cake flour
6 egg whites
1 tsp vanilla extract
3 tbsp (40 g) granulated sugar
¾ cup + 2 tbsp | 85 g sliced (flaked) blanched almonds
1 cup | 300 g apricot jam

Equipment

Piping bag fitted with a ½-inch | 10-mm plain tip

1 ••• Sift the confectioners' sugar into a large bowl. Combine with the ground almonds and flour.
In another large clean, dry bowl, whip the egg whites to a foam. Once they are white and frothy, add the vanilla extract and granulated sugar, and continue to whip until firm.

2 ••• Using a rubber spatula, gently fold the mixture of confectioners' sugar, ground almonds and flour into the whipped egg whites. Start with the spatula in the center of the bowl, work up the sides of the bowl and bring the mixture back down towards the center, all the while turning the bowl regularly. Continue until you have a smooth and homogenous mixture.

•••

3 ••· Preheat the oven to 350°F | 180°C | gas mark 4.
Transfer batter to the piping bag fitted with a plain tip. On a baking sheet lined with parchment paper, pipe small disks, approximately ¾-inch | 2-cm diameter. Sprinkle with sliced almonds. Lower the oven temperature to 340°F | 170°C | gas mark 3. Place sheet in oven and bake for 12 to 15 minutes.
Remove from the oven. Allow to cool completely and dust lightly with confectioners' sugar.

4 ••· Turn every other biscuit upside down.
Place a coin of apricot jam on the biscuit shells resting upside down, and top each with remaining shells.

Chef's tips

Place the biscuits in an airtight container in the refrigerator and allow to rest for a minimum of 12 hours before tasting.
You can also make this recipe using raspberry jam.

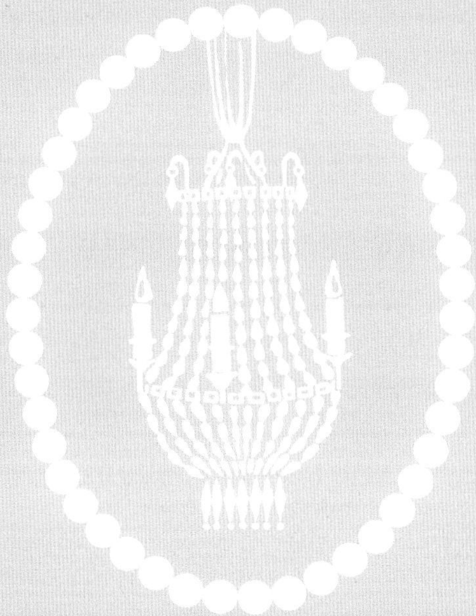

Makes 24 ladyfingers
Preparation: 20 minutes *Cooking time: 15 minutes* *Resting time: 10 minutes*

Biscuits à la Cuillère

Ladyfingers

½ cup | 60 g all-purpose flour
⅓ cup | 60 g potato starch
5 eggs
½ cup + 2 tbsp | 125 g granulated sugar
¼ cup | 30 g confectioners' (icing) sugar

Equipment
Piping bag fitted with a ½-inch | 10-mm plain tip

1 ••• Sift together the flour and potato starch.
Separate the egg whites and yolks.

2 ••• In a large bowl, whisk the egg yolks with half of the sugar until pale. In another large dry bowl, with a clean whisk, bring the egg whites to a foam. Once they are white and frothy, add the remaining half of the sugar and continue to whip until firm.

3 ••• Right away, gently fold the sugar and egg yolk mixture into the whipped egg whites with a rubber spatula. Sprinkle the flour and potato starch over the mixture. Gently combine: start with the spatula in the center of the bowl, work up the sides of the bowl and bring the mixture back down towards the center, all the while turning the bowl regularly. Continue until you have a smooth and homogenous mixture.

•••

4 ••· Transfer batter to the piping bag fitted with a plain tip. On a baking sheet lined with parchment paper, pipe strips 2 ⅓ x ¾-inch | 6 x 2-cm. Preheat oven to 340°F | 170°C | gas mark 3.

5 ••· Using a fine mesh sieve or sifter, sprinkle half of the confectioners' sugar over the piped batter. Allow to rest for 10 minutes and dust the tops again with the remaining confectioners' sugar. Immediately place sheet in oven and bake for approximately 15 minutes until ladyfingers are lightly coloured.
Remove from oven and allow to cool.

Makes 20 to 22 meringues *Preparation: 20 minutes* *Cooking time: 2 ½ hours*

Meringues

Meringues

1 cup | 120 g confectioners' (icing) sugar
4 egg whites
½ cup + 2 tbsp | 120 g granulated sugar

Equipment
Electric mixer fitted with whisk attachment
Piping bag fitted with a ½-inch | 10-mm star tip

1 ••• Preheat the oven to 210°F | 100°C | gas mark ¼.
Sift the confectioners' sugar.

2 ••• In a clean, dry bowl, whip the egg whites to a foam using an electric mixer. Once they are frothy, add roughly 3 tbsp (40 g) of granulated sugar and continue to whip until firm. Add another 3 tbsp (40 g) of granulated sugar and whip for 1 minute. Pour in the remaining 3 tbsp (40 g) of granulated sugar and whip for 1 more minute. Using a rubber spatula, gently fold in the sifted confectioners' sugar.

3 ••• Transfer meringue to the piping bag fitted with a star tip. On a baking sheet lined with parchment paper, pipe twists of meringue. Be sure to leave enough space between meringues as they will spread and rise during baking. If you do not have a piping bag and tip, use two spoons dipped in hot water to shape quenelles (3-sided ovals).

4 ••• Place sheet in oven and bake for approximately 2 ½ hours. The meringues should bake slowly and gradually dry out. Watch that they do not darken too quickly.
Allow to cool completely and store in an airtight container.

Chef's tip
Dust the tops of meringues with confectioners' sugar and serve with ice cream or sorbet.

Makes approximately 50 tuiles   Preparation: 20 minutes   Cooking time: 5 minutes

Tuiles aux Amandes

Almond Tuiles

⅔ cup | 80 g cake flour
2 cups + 1 tbsp | 250 g confectioners' (icing) sugar
1 egg + 5 egg whites
1 tsp vanilla extract
7 tbsp | 100 g butter
+ 1 ½ tbsp butter for baking sheet
2 ¾ cups | 250 g sliced (flaked) blanched almonds

EQUIPMENT

Tuile mould or rolling pin

1 ••• Sift together the flour and confectioners' sugar into a large bowl. Using a wooden spoon, gradually incorporate the egg, egg whites and vanilla extract.
In a small saucepan (or in the microwave), melt the butter and add to the mixture. Stir to combine.
Using a rubber spatula, carefully fold in the sliced almonds. Avoid overmixing, which will break the almonds.

2 ••• Preheat the oven to 350°F | 180°C | gas mark 4.
Using a spoon dipped in water, scoop out batter and drop onto a buttered baking sheet with your index finger. Leave enough space between tuiles, as they will slightly spread during baking. With a fork dipped in cold water, flatten and spread each tuile by lightly pressing down and creating rounds of equal thickness.

•••

3 ••• If you do not have a tuile mould, prepare the rolling pin to give tuiles their curved shape. Lightly oil the rolling pin and place on a creased dish towel to keep from rolling.
Place baking sheet in oven and bake for approximately 5 minutes. Watch tuiles as they bake, and as soon as the edges are golden (the edges will brown faster than the centers), remove from oven.

4 ••• Quickly remove each hot tuile with a metal spatula, place in tuile mould or drape over rolling pin and press down lightly to shape. Do this with each tuile and as soon as it sets, transfer to a cooling rack. Handle carefully as the baked tuiles are very fragile. If the tuiles harden on the baking sheet before being shaped, return them to the oven for a minute or so to soften.

5 ••• Allow to cool completely and store in an airtight container.

Variations

As soon as the tuiles are cool, coat with dark or milk chocolate that has been tempered by the technique below, and then allow to harden.
Melted, tempered chocolate can be quite technical. Here is a simple method: using a knife, chop chocolate on a cutting board. Place in a heatproof bowl set over a pan of gently simmering water to melt. Pour ¾ of this chocolate mass onto a clean, dry work surface. Using an offset stainless steel spatula, spread melted chocolate out, gather together and work back and forth until it starts to thicken. Return to bowl with remaining ¼ of melted chocolate and mix well to homogenize. The tempered chocolate is used at 86°F to 88°F | 30°C to 31°C. Too hot or too cold and it will bloom (turn white) when cooled.
Once the tuiles are coated in this tempered chocolate, allow to set and store in an airtight container.

Chef's tip
You can also allow the tuiles to cool on a flat surface (instead of on a rolling pin). They will be less fragile and easier to store.

LES BOISSONS

Drinks

For 8 people   Preparation: 20 minutes

Chocolat Chaud

Hot Chocolate

1 quart | 1 litre whole milk, cold
⅔ cup | 150 ml water
½ cup | 100 g granulated sugar
6 ½ oz | 185 g bitter chocolate (67% cacao solids)
2 oz | 50 g bitter chocolate
(minimum 80% cacao solids)

1 ••• In a saucepan, bring the milk, water and sugar to a boil. Chop all of the chocolate into small pieces.

2 ••• Remove saucepan from heat and whisk in the chopped chocolate. Whip hot chocolate with an immersion hand blender directly in saucepan (off heat), or transfer to a stand blender and blend until homogenous.

Chef's tips

If you like thick hot chocolate: after adding the chopped chocolate to the milk, put the saucepan back over low heat and bring to a simmer, stirring constantly with a whisk so that the liquid does not stick to the pan. Remove from heat and blend as indicated above.
If you find the hot chocolate too thick when drinking, you can simply add a drop of hot milk.
Once prepared, this hot chocolate keeps very well in the refrigerator for up to 2 days. Pour into an airtight container to store. Reheat in a heatproof bowl over a pan of gently simmering water.
It can also be enjoyed as a cold drink; thin the hot chocolate by adding 1 ¼ cups | 300 ml of cold milk and blend together.

Café Viennois

Viennese Coffee

1 large cup of coffee (long double espresso)
3 tbsp (25 g) sweetened whipped cream: see basic recipe

1 ••• Prepare the sweetened whipped cream in advance and keep in the refrigerator.

2 ••• Prepare the coffee and pour into a large cup.
Using a spoon or a piping bag fitted with a ½-inch | 14-mm star tip, pipe a rosette of sweetened whipped cream on top. Serve immediately.

Chef's tip
Viennese coffee is generally a rather mild coffee topped with unsweetened whipped cream.

For 2 people   Preparation: 10 minutes   Resting time: 5 minutes

Café Blanc aux Trois Agrumes

Triple Citrus Infusion

1 lemon, unwaxed
1 lime, unwaxed
1 orange, unwaxed
2 cups | 450 ml water
2 tbsp (30 g) orange flower water

EQUIPMENT
Grater
Infusion sachets

1 ••· Using a grater, zest the 3 citrus fruits to remove only the coloured part of the rind. Avoid grating the bitter white pith underneath.

2 ••· Mix an equal quantity of grated zest from each fruit.
Fill an infusion sachet with a heaping teaspoon of mixed zest.

3 ••· Bring the water to a simmer and pour into a pot that can be covered. Add the orange flower water and then the infusion sachet. Cover and allow to steep for 5 minutes. Serve.

Makes 1 milkshake   *Preparation: 5 minutes*

Milkshake

Milkshake

2 scoops of vanilla ice cream
½ cup | 120 ml whole milk, cold

EQUIPMENT
Blender
Mazagran or other serving glass

1 ••• Remove ice cream from freezer 10 minutes in advance to soften.

2 ••• Put scoops of ice cream in a blender and pour in the cold milk. Blend together until smooth.
Pour into serving glass and serve immediately.

Chef's tip
If you do not have a stand blender, you can also prepare the milkshake using an immersion hand blender.

VARIATION

This recipe can be used with all flavours of ice cream: coffee, chocolate, caramel...
For fruit milkshakes, strawberry for example, add ⅓ cup | 50 g of fruit and blend with the milk and ice cream.

Les Recettes de Base

Basic Recipes

Makes 16 oz | 450 g of dough
Preparation: 20 minutes *Resting time: minimum of 2 hours, ideally 12 hours*

Pâte Sucrée aux Amandes

Sweet Almond Pastry

½ cup | 120 g butter, very cold
½ cup + 1 tbsp | 70 g confectioners' (icing) sugar
¼ cup | 25 g ground almonds (almond flour)
1 pinch of fleur de sel (or other coarse sea salt)
1 pinch of vanilla powder (or a few drops of vanilla extract) (optional)
1 egg
1 ⅔ cups | 200 g cake flour

1 ••• Sift the confectioners' sugar. Cut the butter into small pieces and place in a bowl. (Or, if you have a stand mixer, place in the bowl of the mixer fitted with the paddle attachment.) Work the butter to homogenize and then add the following ingredients, one by one, making sure to fully incorporate each into the mixture before the next addition: sifted confectioners' sugar, ground almonds, fleur de sel, vanilla, egg and flour. Combine ingredients just until the dough comes together; do not overwork the dough. This will give the pastry its desired crumbly texture.

2 ••• Form the dough into a ball and wrap in plastic wrap. Refrigerate for a minimum of 2 hours before using. If possible, it is better to prepare the dough one day ahead; it will be easier to roll out.

Chef's tip

This recipe makes 16 oz | 450 g of dough, and the final texture depends entirely on the proportions that go with 1 egg. Therefore, I suggest you make the entire recipe even if you do not need that much dough. If you have left over, you can roll it out to ⅒ inch | 2 mm thick, without adding too much flour when working with it. Cut out small biscuits, 1 ¼ x 1 ¼-inch | 3 x 3-cm squares or ¾ x 1 ½-inch | 2 x 4-cm rectangles. Otherwise, keep unrolled dough in the refrigerator for a maximum of 5 days for another use.

Makes dough for 1 tart for 8 people   *Preparation: 20 minutes*   *Resting time: 1 hour*

Pâte Brisée

Shortcrust Pastry (Basic Tart Dough)

2 cups | 250 g cake flour
9 tbsp | 125 g butter, very cold
1 pinch of fleur de sel (or other coarse sea salt)
4 tbsp water
2 egg yolks

1 ••• Sift the flour into a large bowl. Cut the chilled butter into very small pieces and add to bowl, along with the fleur de sel. Using the palms of your hands, work the butter into the flour and salt until it resembles small grain or sand.

2 ••• When the mixture has this texture, add the water and egg yolks. Incorporate into the butter and flour mixture just until the dough is homogenous and holds together; do not overwork the dough.
(If you have a stand mixer, you can prepare the dough in the bowl of the mixer fitted with the paddle attachment.)

3 ••• Form the dough into a ball and wrap in plastic wrap. Refrigerate for a minimum of 1 hour before using. You can also prepare the dough one day ahead; it will be easier to roll out.

Makes about 2 lbs | 1 kg of dough   *Preparation: 30 minutes*   *Resting time: 9 hours*

Pâte Feuilletée

Puff Pastry

2 ½ tsp (10 g) fleur de sel (or other coarse sea salt)
1 cup | 250 ml water
5 tbsp | 75 g butter
+ 1 ½ cups + 4 tbsp | 400 g butter, very cold
4 cups | 500 g cake flour

1 ••• Dissolve the fleur de sel in the water at room temperature.
In a small saucepan, melt the 5 tbsp | 75 g of butter over low heat.
Place the flour in a large bowl, incorporate the water and salt mixture, and then add the melted butter. Mix together using your fingertips, just until the dough is homogenous and holds together; do not overwork the dough.

2 ••• Gather the dough (called the détrempe), place on a clean work surface and form into a 6 x 6-inch | 15 x 15-cm square. Wrap in plastic wrap and refrigerate for 1 hour until firm.

3 ••• Put the 1 ½ cups + 4 tbsp | 400 g of chilled butter onto a sheet of parchment paper. Using a rolling pin, pound on the butter to soften it.
Using the parchment paper to help you, fold the butter back on itself and continue to soften it. It must have the same consistency as the dough.
Form the butter into a 6 x 6-inch | 15 x 15-cm square (called the beurrage).
If necessary, allow the détrempe to sit at room temperature to soften, or

chill the beurrage briefly to harden.
Roll out the détrempe to obtain a 12 x 12-inch | 30 x 30-cm square and place the beurrage in the center on a diagonal. Fold the 4 corners of the dough into the center, to completely enclose the butter. No part of the butter should be exposed.

4 ••• Roll out this package of dough to a rectangle 24 inches | 60 cm long, and then fold it in thirds (like a business letter). Give this folded dough (called the pâton) a one quarter turn, roll it out again to a length of 24 inches | 60 cm, and once again fold it in thirds. Each time you fold in thirds, you have completed a single turn. You should turn the dough a total of 6 times, allowing the dough to rest for 2 hours in the refrigerator after every 2 turns.

5 ••• Once you have completed the 6 turns, allow the dough to rest in the refrigerator for a minimum of 2 hours, or ideally overnight. Keep in the refrigerator until ready to use.

Preparation: 30 minutes *Cooking time: 33 minutes*

Pâte Feuilletée Caramélisée

Caramelized Puff Pastry

about 2 lbs | 1 kg puff pastry dough: see recipe, page 360
1 ½ tbsp butter for baking sheet
⅓ cup | 50 g all-purpose flour for work surface
1 ¼ cups | 150 g confectioners' (icing) sugar

1 ••• Butter a baking sheet and line with parchment paper. Press the paper down onto the butter, so it will stay in place on the sheet.

2 ••• Preheat the oven to 330°F | 165°C | gas mark 3.
On a floured work surface, roll out the puff pastry dough to a thickness of ⅒ inch | 2 mm at most, giving it the same shape as the baking sheet. Transfer the dough to the baking sheet and cover with another sheet of parchment paper. Place a wire rack or another baking sheet on top to prevent the pastry from puffing up too much while baking.

3 ••• Place in oven and bake for 25 to 30 minutes until the pastry is uniformly baked and lightly golden. Remove from oven and allow to cool completely.

4 ••• Preheat the oven to 465°F | 240°C | gas mark 9. Sprinkle a thin, even layer of confectioners' sugar over the baked pastry. Bake again for 2 to 3 minutes, keeping a close eye on the pastry, as the cooking time is very short. When the sugar has melted, immediately remove from oven.

Chef's tip

Allow the puff pastry to cool completely before baking it a second time. The sugar will then be able to caramelize without the pastry underneath it baking again and becoming too dark.

Makes 7 oz | 200 g of dough   Preparation: 20 minutes
Cooking time: 15 to 20 minutes   Resting time: 1 hour and 20 minutes

Pâte Sablée Croustillante à Crumble

Crisp Sweet Pastry for Crumbles

3 ½ tbsp | 50 g butter, very cold
⅓ cup | 50 g all-purpose flour
+ 2 ½ tbsp all-purpose flour for work surface
¼ cup | 50 g granulated sugar
½ cup | 50 g ground almonds (almond flour)
1 pinch of salt

1 ••• Cut the chilled butter into small pieces. Sift the flour into a large bowl and add the butter, sugar, ground almonds and salt. Using the palms of your hands, work the ingredients just until the dough comes together.

2 ••• Form the dough into a ball and wrap in plastic wrap. Refrigerate for a minimum of 1 hour before using.

3 ••• On a floured work surface, roll out the dough to a thickness of approximately ⅕ inch | 5 mm.
Cut ⅓-inch | 1-cm cubes. Refrigerate for 20 minutes to harden.

4 ••• Preheat the oven to 300°F | 150°C | gas mark 2.
Place the pastry cubes on a baking sheet lined with parchment paper. Spread them out on the sheet, making sure to separate any pieces that stick together.
Place sheet in oven and bake for 15 to 20 minutes until golden.
Allow to cool completely and store in an airtight container.

Chef's tip
You can also prepare the dough one day ahead (steps 1 and 2) and bake the following day.

Makes dough for 10 éclairs, 10 gourmet delights, 25 small cream puffs or 25 salambos
Preparation: 20 minutes   Cooking time: 3 minutes

Pâte à Choux

Choux Pastry (Cream Puff Dough)

1 cup - ½ tbsp | 120 g cake flour
½ cup - 1 tbsp | 100 ml whole milk
½ cup - 1 tbsp | 100 ml water
1 tbsp (10 g) granulated sugar
1 pinch of salt
5 ½ tbsp | 80 g butter
4 eggs

1 ••• Sift the flour. In a saucepan, bring the milk, water, sugar, salt and butter to a boil. Remove from heat. Incorporate the sifted flour into the hot liquid, mixing energetically with a spatula until homogenous. Return the saucepan to low heat and stir vigorously for 1 minute to pull out the moisture from the batter, so that it forms a mass and pulls away from the sides of the pan.

2 ••• Transfer batter to a large bowl and allow to cool. Add the eggs one at a time, carefully incorporating each into the batter with a spatula.

3 ••• When homogenous, pipe into the desired form for cream puffs, éclairs, salambos, etc.

Makes 26 oz | 750 g of dough *Preparation: 25 minutes* *Resting time: 5 hours*

Pâte à Brioche

Brioche Dough

2 ¼ cups | 280 g cake flour
3 tbsp (40 g) granulated sugar
1 tsp (5 g) salt
⅓ oz | 10 g fresh yeast
4 eggs
12 ½ tbsp | 180 g butter

1 ••• Place the flour in a large bowl. Add the sugar and salt, placing on one side of the flour and the fresh yeast broken up in little pieces (using your fingers) on the other side. Important: the yeast must not come in contact with the sugar and salt before you start to mix the dough; otherwise it will lose its properties.

2 ••• Cut the butter into small pieces.
In a bowl, beat the eggs. Pour ⅔ of the eggs over the flour and begin by mixing all ingredients together with a wooden spatula. Incorporate the remaining third of the eggs little by little. Knead the dough with your hands, until it starts to pull away from the sides of the bowl. Add the butter and continue to work the dough until it once again pulls away from the sides of the bowl.

3 ••• Transfer the dough to a clean large bowl and cover with a damp dish towel or plastic wrap, and keep at room temperature. Allow the dough to

double in volume (approximately 2 ½ hours).
Return the dough to its initial volume by folding it back on itself.

4 ••• Refrigerate the dough for 2 ½ hours; while chilling, it will once again rise. Deflate it again by folding it back on itself. The dough is then ready to use.

Chef's tips

If you have a stand mixer, make this dough in the bowl of the mixer fitted with the dough hook attachment.
This recipe will yield dough for 12 individual brioches (2 oz | 60 g) or 14 brioches (1 ¾ oz | 50 g).
It can also make 24 mini brioches (1 oz | 30 g).

Makes 5 cups | 600 g of pastry cream *Preparation: 30 minutes* *Cooking time: 5 minutes*

Crème Pâtissière

Pastry Cream

1 vanilla bean
1 ⅔ cups | 400 ml whole milk
4 egg yolks
½ cup - 1 tbsp | 80 g granulated sugar
¼ cup | 30 g cornstarch (cornflour)
2 tbsp | 25 g butter

Chef's tips

Be sure to keep a close eye on the milk as it heats to avoid overflows, which can be quite common. Also make sure that the saucepan is covered tightly while the vanilla steeps in the milk, to prevent any water from evaporating. Without this precaution, the recipe could fail, as the cream will be too dry.

1 ••• With a sharp knife, slice the vanilla bean in half lengthwise. Using the tip, scrape the interior to remove the seeds. Pour the milk into a saucepan and add the vanilla pod and seeds. Bring to a simmer.
Remove from heat, cover immediately and allow to infuse for 15 minutes.

2 ••• In a large bowl, whisk the egg yolks and sugar until slightly pale. Incorporate the cornstarch.
Remove the vanilla pod from the saucepan and reheat the milk, bringing to a simmer. Pour a third of the hot milk over the egg yolk, sugar and cornstarch mixture (to temper the yolks). Whisk together and pour the whole mixture back into the saucepan. Bring to a boil while stirring with a whisk, making sure to scrape down the sides of the pan with a spatula.

3 ••• Remove from heat and pour the cream into a clean bowl. Allow to cool for 10 minutes so that it is still hot but not boiling. Incorporate the butter while stirring. Cover the bowl with plastic wrap until ready to use.

Makes 12 oz | 350 g of almond cream *Preparation: 20 minutes*

Crème d'Amandes

Almond Cream

7 tbsp | 100 g butter
¾ cup | 100 g confectioners' (icing) sugar
1 cup | 100 g ground almonds (almond flour)
1 tbsp (10 g) cornstarch (cornflour)
2 eggs
1 tbsp rum

1 ••• Cut the butter into small pieces and put in a large heatproof bowl. Place over a pan of gently simmering water or in the microwave to soften until creamy, without allowing it to melt.

2 ••• Incorporate the following ingredients into the butter, making sure to mix well after each addition: confectioners' sugar, ground almonds, cornstarch, eggs and rum.

Chef's tip

So that the almond cream has a smooth texture, prepare it just before using.

Crème Chantilly

Sweetened Whipped Cream (Chantilly)

1 ¼ cups | 300 ml heavy (double) cream, very cold
3 tbsp (25 g) confectioners' (icing) sugar

1 ••• Keep the heavy cream in the refrigerator until ready to use. It must be very cold in order to whip.

2 ••• Place a large mixing bowl in the freezer to chill.

3 ••• Pour the very cold cream into the chilled bowl and whisk energetically. As soon as it thickens, add the sugar and continue to whip until the cream is firm.

Makes about 2 cups | 500 ml of pouring custard
Preparation: 40 minutes   Cooking time: 10 minutes

Crème Anglaise

Pouring Custard

2 vanilla beans
1 cup + 1 tbsp | 250 ml whole milk
1 cup + 1 tbsp | 250 ml heavy (double) cream
6 egg yolks
½ cup | 100 g granulated sugar

1 ••• With a sharp knife, slice the vanilla beans in half lengthwise. Using the tip, scrape the interior to remove the seeds. Pour the milk and cream into a saucepan and add the vanilla pods and seeds. Bring to a simmer. Remove from heat, cover immediately and allow to infuse for 15 minutes.

2 ••• In a large bowl, whisk the egg yolks and sugar until slightly pale. Remove the vanilla pods from the milk and cream mixture and reheat the liquid, bringing to a simmer. Pour a third of this hot liquid over the egg yolks and sugar (to temper the yolks). Whisk together and pour the whole mixture back into the saucepan.

3 ••• Cook over low heat, stirring constantly with a wooden spoon until the mixture thickens. It should coat the spoon when ready; if you run your finger down the back of the spoon, the custard should not run back into the line. Important: the custard should never come to a boil. (It should cook at a maximum of 185°F | 85°C.)

•••

4 ••• As soon as the custard has this consistency, remove from heat and pour into a large bowl to stop the cooking. Continue to stir for 5 minutes so that the custard stays smooth.
Allow to cool completely and keep in the refrigerator to serve very cold.

Chef's tip

If you let the custard cook a little too long, lumps will appear. This is due to the egg yolks that are beginning to curdle. To save it, pour the custard into a blender or food processor and briefly blend just to homogenize. Do not blend too long or the custard will liquefy.

Makes 14 oz | 400 g of mousseline cream
Preparation: 20 minutes *Resting time: 20 minutes*

Crème Mousseline Pistache

Pistachio Mousseline Cream

6 ½ tbsp | 90 g butter
¾ cup | 180 ml whole milk
2 egg yolks
¼ cup | 50 g granulated sugar
2 tbsp (15 g) cornstarch (cornflour)
¼ cup | 60 g pistachio paste

1 ••• Remove the butter from the refrigerator to soften.
In a saucepan, bring the milk to a simmer.

2 ••• In a large bowl, whisk the egg yolks and sugar until slightly pale. Incorporate the cornstarch. Pour a third of the hot milk over the mixture of egg yolks, sugar and cornstarch (to temper the yolks). Whisk together and pour the whole mixture back into the saucepan. Bring to a boil while stirring with a whisk, making sure to scrape down the sides of the pan with a spatula.

3 ••• Remove from heat and allow to cool for 10 minutes so that it is hot but not boiling. Incorporate half of the butter. Pour into a baking dish, cover with plastic wrap and allow to cool.
The cream should be at room temperature (64°F to 68°F | 18°C to 20°C). If it is still hot, refrigerate for 10 minutes to finish cooling off.

4 ••• In a large bowl, whip the mousseline cream with an electric mixer until smooth. Add the pistachio paste and the remaining half of the butter. Whip to emulsify the mixture until smooth.

Makes approximately 30 oz | 850 g of mousseline cream
Preparation: 30 minutes   Resting time: 20 minutes

Crème Mousseline au Praliné

Praline Mousseline Cream

½ cup + 5 tbsp | 185 g butter
1 ½ cups + 2 tbsp | 380 ml whole milk
3 egg yolks
½ cup + 2 tbsp | 120 g granulated sugar
¼ cup | 35 g cornstarch (cornflour)
3 oz | 90 g almond praline paste
1 oz | 35 g hazelnut praline paste

1 ••• Remove the butter from the refrigerator to soften.
In a saucepan, bring the milk to a simmer.

2 ••• In a large bowl, whisk the egg yolks and sugar until slightly pale. Incorporate the cornstarch. Pour a third of the hot milk over the mixture of egg yolks, sugar and cornstarch (to temper the yolks). Whisk together and pour the whole mixture back into the saucepan. Bring to a boil while stirring with a whisk, making sure to scrape down the sides of the pan with a spatula.

3 ••• Remove from heat and allow to cool for 10 minutes so that it is hot but not boiling. Incorporate half of the butter. Pour into a baking dish, cover with plastic wrap and allow to cool.
The cream should be at room temperature (64°F to 68°F | 18°C to 20°C). If it is still hot, refrigerate for 10 minutes to finish cooling off.

4 ••• In a large bowl, whip the mousseline cream with an electric mixer until smooth. Add the praline pastes and the remaining half of the butter. Whip to emulsify the mixture until smooth.

Makes 1 cup | 250 ml of coulis *Preparation: 15 minutes*

Coulis de Fraises

Strawberry Coulis

2 cups | 300 g strawberries, hulled
2 ½ tbsp (30 g) granulated sugar
2 tbsp lemon juice
2 tbsp water

1 ••• In a blender or food processor, blend the strawberries with the sugar until you have a liquid consistency.

2 ••• Strain the mixture through a fine mesh sieve; alternate pressing and scraping with a spoon to obtain as much pulp as possible without the strawberry seeds (akenes).
To make this easier, just before all of the strawberry puree has been strained, add the 2 tbsp of lemon juice and the 2 tbsp of water to the sieve, which will pass through with any remaining strawberry pulp.

3 ••• Keep the coulis in the refrigerator.

Chef's tip
Served chilled, this coulis is a great accompaniment to strawberries sprinkled with sugar, a fruit cake, vanilla ice cream or strawberry sorbet.

Makes 1 cup | 250 ml of coulis *Preparation: 15 minutes*

Coulis de Framboises

Raspberry Coulis

2 ¼ cups | 300 g raspberries
2 ½ tbsp (30 g) granulated sugar
2 tbsp lemon juice
3 tbsp water

1 ••• In a blender or food processor, blend the raspberries with the sugar until you have a liquid consistency.

2 ••• Strain the mixture through a fine mesh sieve; alternate pressing and scraping with a spoon to obtain as much pulp as possible without the raspberry seeds.
To make this easier, just before all of the raspberry puree has been strained, add the 2 tbsp of lemon juice and the 3 tbsp of water to the sieve, which will pass through with any remaining raspberry pulp.

3 ••• Keep the coulis in the refrigerator.

Chef's tip
This coulis is a great accompaniment to all fruit cakes, which I recommend serving with ice cream or sorbet.

Makes 1 cup | 250 ml of coulis   Preparation: 20 minutes

Coulis de Passion

Passion Fruit Coulis

½ banana
2 oranges
1 ½ tbsp (20 g) granulated sugar
12 passion fruits

1 ••• Peel the banana half and chop into pieces. Juice the oranges. Using an immersion hand blender or food processor, blend together the chopped banana, orange juice and sugar until you have a liquid consistency.

2 ••• Using a spoon, remove the pulp and seeds from the passion fruits. You can leave the seeds in the coulis if you would like – the result is more attractive – or you can discard them. If you choose to remove the seeds, strain through a fine mesh sieve; alternate pressing and scraping with a spoon to obtain as much pulp as possible without the seeds.

3 ••• Add the passion fruit pulp to the banana and orange juice mixture and blend. Keep the coulis in the refrigerator.

Chef's tip

Passion fruits are unfortunately not always full of juice. That is why I add the orange juice to make it more liquid and the banana to give it a nice texture.

Index

RECIPES

BASIC RECIPES

Philippe Andrieu

PASTRY CHEF

Using all that he had learned on his travels and with the strong influence of Michel Bras, Philippe Andrieu expresses himself fully as Pastry Chef at world-renown Ladurée. Driven by his desire to give pleasure to others, he allows his creativity to flow by marrying tastes and textures (soft, melting, crunchy, crisp).

Born in Figeac, Philippe spent his childhood in Saint-Cirgues in the Lot, a southwestern region of France. It was by cooking with his mother and helping with service at the family's restaurant, that his desire to go to culinary school grew. He left for the *École Hôtelière* in Souillac at the age of 15. Step by step, from service to the kitchen, he earned his degree in cooking and gradually discovered his passion… pastry. After quickly getting a taste of the rigours of the fundamentals of pastry, he ultimately received his degree in pastry.

He began his career in gastronomic restaurants as a pastry cook. At the age of 20, after four weeks of military training duties, he then completed his military service as kitchen manager in the officers' mess in Toulouse. After the army, he left to work in Michelin-starred restaurants, and most notably, that of Georges Blanc and then Michel Bras. It was with Michel Bras that he first truly learned the art of creation. Working beside the starred chef of Laguiole, Andrieu was enthused by the *biscuit de chocolat fondant* and the *millefeuille à la nougatine au beurre et à la crème fromagère.*

There only for the summer, he left during the winter to work in the restaurant La Bourgogne Relais Châteaux in Punta del Este in Uruguay. For three years he divided his time between Uruguay and France. During the two years that followed, he opened two pastry shops for a French brand in Korea (in Seoul and Busan), as well as one in Hong Kong and another in Cairo, while also giving pastry demos in Japan.

The time finally came for Philippe Andrieu to settle down; he thus accepted the title of Pastry Chef at Ladurée, taking the helm of the test kitchens. In addition to controlling logistics, management and ongoing training of the personnel, he also succeeded in evolving the diverse pastry repertoire of Ladurée. His first creations of the chocolate macaron and assorted pastries quickly became Ladurée classics: rhubarb and wild strawberry tart, Harmonie and Élysée cakes, blackcurrant-violet macaron, caramel macaron with fleur de sel, chocolate candies with cacao bean nougatine, macaron chocolates…

Acknowledgements

Ladurée gives warm thanks to all of its teams, and most especially to Philippe Andrieu for his recipes and creations, to Bertrand Bernier in charge of the overall organization of the test kitchen, to Nicolas Ledoux and Willy Meunier for making the pastries and to Patrick Sallaberry and Stéphanie Vincent for preparing the written recipes. Ladurée also gives thanks to station chefs Julien Christophe, Franck Lenoir, Rodolphe Benoit and Muriel Nau, and to the communications department: Safia Thomass-Bendali, Aude Schlosser and Hanako Schiano.

Christèle Ageorges and Sophie Tramier thank Véronique Villaret for her magnificent porcelain creations.

Coloured paper and fabrics: Au Fil des Couleurs/Mauny, Sanderson, Osborne and Little, Les Beaux Draps de Jeannine Cros, Brunschwig et Fils, Designers Guild, Canovas, Farrow and Ball, La Cerise sur le Gâteau

Tableware: Véronique Villaret, The Conran Shop, Astier de Villatte, Mis en Demeure, Sandrine Ganem, 107 Rivoli, Le Bon Marché, Reichenbach, Wedgwood, Tsé-Tsé/Sentou Galerie, Christiane Perrochon/La Forge Subtile, Laurence Brabant, Caroline Swift, La Boutique, Jars Céramiques, Marc Albert/ Ateliers d'Art, Marie Verlet Nezri

Colours: Tollens
Friezes: Sedap
Flowers: Marianne Robic

METRIC AND IMPERIAL CONVERSIONS

WEIGHT

Metric	Imperial
28 g	1 oz
450 g	1 lb
1 kg	2.2 lbs

LIQUID VOLUME

Metric	Imperial
5 ml	1 tsp
15 ml	1 tbsp
30 ml	1 fl oz
600 ml	1 pint (20 fl oz)
1 litre	1 ¾ pints (35 fl oz)

Translation by Kerrin Rousset
Editorial Manager : Valérie Tognali – Cécile Beaucourt
Artistic director: Sabine Houplain
Layout design: Marie-Paule Jaulme
Layout: Vincent Lanceau
Production: Amandine Sevestre

ISBN: 978-2-81230-443-9
NUART : 34/2605/3-08

Printed in China

First published, in French, by
Editions du Chêne-Hachette Livre, 2009
Original Title:
Maison Fondée en 1862
LADUREE
Fabricant de douceurs
Paris
Sucré